To live authentic, honest lives takes immense courage and humility. Juli opens our hearts to this kind of scandalous living, being willing to look honestly at our pain, our profound brokenness, and our need for God's amazing grace and mercy—which is, as she so beautifully portrays, the only kind of living that matters.

> Tammy Maltby
> Author of *Confessions of a Good Christian Girl*
> and *Lifegiving*
> Cohost of the Emmy-nominated television
> show *Aspiring Women*

In *Beyond the Masquerade* Dr. Julianna Slattery will skillfully and gently guide you into "unveiling the authentic you." She'll help you understand why your self-worth, self-concept, and self-confidence can only be real if they are rooted and grounded in a relationship with the Lord Jesus Christ. You will learn why positive thinking by itself just isn't enough.

If you are tired of wearing a mask, tired of trying to change, and if you are ready to actually do it, keep reading. You will be amazed at the changes and the freedom you will gain through Jesus Christ alone!

> Dr. Bob Barnes
> President, Sheridan House Family Ministries

There is nothing more frightening yet freeing than unmasking. Yet women continue to live in loneliness because the fear overshadows the freedom. Julianna Slattery hits the nail on the head when she talks about the brokenness required for the journey to wholeness. Our *Midday Connection* mailbox is stuffed with letters from women who want true community but don't know how to get there. Want a real roadmap? Read *Beyond the Masquerade*. Better yet, read it together with a small group of women. You'll never be the same.

Anita Lustrea

Host and executive producer, *Midday Connection*

Many voices in today's culture claim that low self-esteem is at the root of every emotional and relational struggle we face. But Juli Slattery argues that we must completely rethink our definition of self-esteem, focusing instead on the true Source of value and purpose in life. Juli brings great wisdom, insight, and biblical understanding to this often-misunderstood topic. She also writes as a trusted friend, sharing openly and honestly from the secret places of her own heart.

If you long to be known, loved, and accepted for who you truly are, you will find freedom and hope in the pages of this book!

Dr. Bill Maier

Vice-president and Psychologist in Residence

Focus on the Family

BEYOND THE MASQUERADE

Tyndale House Publishers, Inc., Carol Stream, IL

Beyond the Masquerade

unveiling the authentic you

Dr. Julianna Slattery

A Focus on the Family book published by
Tyndale House Publishers, Inc., Carol Stream, Illinois 60188

Focus on the Family and the accompanying logo and design are federally registered
trademarks of Focus on the Family, Colorado Springs, CO 80995.

TYNDALE and Tyndale's quill logo are registered trademarks of Tyndale House
Publishers, Inc.

The case examples presented in this book are fictional composites based on the author's
clinical experience with hundreds of clients throughout the years. Any resemblance
between these fictional characters and actual persons is coincidental.

Editor: Kathy Davis
Cover design by: Jennifer Ghionzoli
Cover photograph of mask © by Joy Fera/iStockphoto. All rights reserved.
Cover photograph of woman © by Creatas Images/Alamy. All rights reserved.
Author photograph © by Jim Maguire

Library of Congress Cataloging-in-Publication Data
Slattery, Julianna, 1969-
  Beyond the masquerade : unveiling the authentic you / Julianna Slattery.
     p. cm.
  ISBN-13: 978-1-58997-377-0
  ISBN-10: 1-58997-377-1
  1. Self-esteem—Religious aspects—Christianity. 2. Integrity—Religious aspects—Christian-
ity. I. Title.
  BV4598.24.S53 2007
  248.4—dc22
                                          2007003028

Printed in the United States of America
4 5 6 7 8 9 /13 12 11 10

Contents

To my dad
Your love is a living example of our Father's love!

Acknowledgments

It was such a joy to work with Focus on the Family and Tyndale House on this project. Thank you Kathy Davis, Nanci McAlister, and Larry Weeden for the warm invitation and all the hard work you invested. Special thanks to Bill Maier and Jim Levy for introducing me to the "Focus" family.

Over the past year, many friends and colleagues have read some or all of this manuscript and provided invaluable input. Thanks to Cheryl and Warren Kniskern, Kari Buddenburg, Susan Bebee, Rebecca Stephonic, Pam Rybka, Stephanie Hall, Stephanie Massa, Sue Burnham, Claudia Bosshard, Susan Bissonette, and Anne Stancil for your time, feedback, and prayers. Typing into a keyboard in the middle of the night can get lonely. Your companionship was precious.

Thanks to Vicky Popp and Amanda Helin for keeping me organized. You both know how much I needed your help!

Special thanks to Kim Bush and Susie Sartarelli for your prayers and encouragement when I doubted. Kim, your friendship is a safe place, a rare blessing. Susie, much of this book was born out of our conversations. Thank you for always speaking truth in love.

Among my dearest friends are my five siblings: Larry, Cheryl, Michael, Amy, and Angela. The unspoken bond among us is a comfort and a blessing that our parents began and that the Lord has solidified. I treasure each of you.

Mom and Dad, when I think of all you've given to me, I can't even begin to say thank you. Throughout my lifetime, you've planted and watered the seeds of authenticity in my life and provided shelter and sunshine in due season. Those seeds have grown into the fruit of this labor. I trust and pray that your investment will reap a harvest for eternity.

Finally, my best friend, Mike. Oh, what joy to have been blessed with a husband who loves me when my makeup is off, my hair is sticking up, and my faults are exposed! I marvel at the love you show me. I'm so thankful for the ways God has drawn us closer through all He is teaching us! My bags are packed.

Introduction

The best way to begin writing a nonfiction book is probably to lay out what you want to teach the reader. After all, why write unless you have something profound to impart? Although this was only my third venture as an author, I knew from the beginning that this book would be different. Rather than writing a message that I wanted to teach, I wrote about a lesson that I desperately needed to learn.

As you read this book, you'll quickly realize that I'm not an "expert" so much as someone who is walking alongside you. After all, my credentials are just another form of hiding in the "Masquerade." I'm more convinced than ever that God's truth, wisdom, and power shine through our weaknesses far greater than through our strengths. It's only when we're lacking that we're driven to our knees to seek Him.

I've spent my life in the evangelical church. Although my heritage is a tremendous blessing, I also realize how crippled the Western church is. So many of our efforts to reach and please God are strangled in an obsession with self. The problem isn't a new one. The demon of pride has taken on many different faces throughout the history of humankind. However, this present danger is tenfold because we fail to recognize it as a problem.

The gospel of John records Jesus' teaching on how God prunes our branches so that we might bear more fruit.[1] I always understood this as referring to how God cuts away the bad things in our lives: lust, gossip, materialism, foul language—they all have to be discarded. Now I understand that God also prunes away branches that may actually look good and fruitful to us. Many things I once considered "spiritual" I now see as hindering my dependence on Him.

Ambition, family, popularity, busyness, friendliness, success, self-confidence, perfectionism—these are good things that can make our Christian lives fruitful. After all, we reach neighbors by hosting parties in our perfect homes. We impress educators by flawlessly teaching our children. We build beautiful churches with the money we've earned through our hard work. We may even raise well-behaved children and maintain intimate marriages. However, we're continually at risk of placing trust in what we do—even in what we believe we're doing for God.

In the quiet of the night, I hear the question, *Juli, are you serving Me or am I serving you? Who is glorified through the good things you do?*

There are no "10 steps" to pure motives and authenticity. Authenticity isn't a goal we can achieve through effort but rather something that pursues us as we surrender more to the King. I can't promise that this will be an easy book to read. It wasn't easy to write. However, I can promise that when God prunes away "good" branches, it's always to make way for something far more fruitful.

God's pruning usually feels painful—sometimes even crippling. It seems crazy to ask for His discipline in our lives. Yet, be encouraged by the words of Hebrews 12:10–13:

> God disciplines us for our good, that we may share in his holiness. No discipline seems pleasant at the time, but

painful. Later on, however, it produces a harvest of righteousness and peace for those who have been trained by it.

Therefore, strengthen your feeble arms and weak knees.
"Make level paths for your feet," so that the lame may not
be disabled, but rather healed.

Does your soul yearn for more of God? Although you fear
the pain of His pruning, do you long to share in His holiness?
Journey with me as He first shows us how "lame" we are in our
own strength and then heals us with the power of His love and
truth.

Your sister in Christ,

Juli

What is most wrong in us is least visible to us.

—DR. LARRY CRABB

1

Welcome to the Masquerade!

Perhaps your morning was like mine. I reluctantly rolled out of bed, feeling the impact of a late night. After stumbling into the bathroom, I groped for the light switch and was rewarded with a brightness that was far too intense for Monday morning. I splashed water on my face and began to brush my teeth. While brushing, I stared at the dark circles under my eyes, chuckled at my wayward hair, and noticed a large red pimple forming on the left side of my nose. Next, I stripped off my clothes, turned on the shower, and stepped on the scale. *Not too bad given my week-end indulgences,* I thought. How a number can determine the tone of my day!

After showering, the real work began. Deodorant, baby powder, mouthwash, and perfume to control offensive odors. Blow-dryer, comb, and styling gel to tame my hair. The face—now that was the ultimate challenge. Since this would be a workday involving human interaction with others beyond my children, I decided on the "medium-level makeover." I started by spreading moisturizer on my face and neck and tweezing stray eyebrow hairs. Next, I applied under-eye concealer, blemish concealer, blush, and powder. I carefully employed eyeliner and mascara to highlight my sunken brown eyes. With a lip pencil, I outlined my bottom lip, literally drew an upper lip since I have none, and then filled it all in with glittering ruby lipstick. After trying on three pairs of dress slacks, I found one that fit comfortably, projected casual professionalism, and matched an ironed blouse. I looked at myself in the mirror and declared myself presentable.

Amazing what it takes to get ready to face the world. Imagine going to church, work, or lunch with a friend simply as you are—no shower, hair matted, no makeup or deodorant. I've had those days—have you? Running late with no time or energy for personal hygiene? Even if it's a quick trip to the grocery store, I'm acutely aware of my disheveled appearance, and I feel completely unprepared for personal interaction.

My 30-minute morning routine is well worth the time and effort. In its natural state, my body stinks, my breath reeks, my skin is blotchy, I have bushy eyebrows and hairy underarms, my lips are too small, and my stomach is too flabby. Wrinkles, gray hair, and varicose veins are just starting to appear, foreshadowing my future decline. Frankly, in this world I need all the cosmetic help I can get.

Although I may not be aware of it, I usually put even more effort, time, and energy into making myself emotionally and relationally presentable. Facing others without covering my psychological blemishes is actually more terrifying than going out into the world without a shower or makeup. Far more offensive than body odor are my fears, malicious thoughts, insecurities, shame, and pride.

Imagine if everyone could see through your smile, scripted words, and confident appearance. What if your boss, your friends, your neighbors, your relatives, the grocery clerk, and your children could peer into your soul and know the depth of who you *really* are—the good, the bad, and the ugly? Perhaps even more threatening, what if you lived with the daily, moment-to-moment awareness of your own deepest pain, shame, and insecurity? Such intimacy, such honesty, such nakedness, such consciousness would be paralyzing. Have you ever felt it? Who has the strength and courage to live so genuinely? Is it even possible?

TO BE HUMAN IS TO BE HIDING

The Phantom of the Opera is one of Broadway's greatest musicals. The play tells the story of a brilliant composer with terrible facial deformities. Throughout his childhood, he was mocked and rejected. As an adult, he developed his genius as a musician and an architect, posing as a ghost who haunts an opera theater. When the Phantom falls in love with one of the young opera singers, the only way he knows how to win her affection is through hypnosis, intimidation, and manipulation. As the story of unrequited love unfolds, the Phantom reveals his life of loneliness and agony. His first piece of clothing as an infant was a mask to hide his horrendous appearance. He was born to be hidden.[1]

Can you relate to the Phantom? When were you first fitted

for a mask? Although you may have been loved and adored as a baby, it probably didn't take long before your "deformities" entered the scene. Do you remember when you were first aware of not being okay, when you first realized that just being you wasn't enough? At what point did the stains of human sin and shame become your reality?

When Kendra was only two, her mother abandoned her. Kendra lived with her father, who soon remarried and had three more children with Kendra's stepmother. Although they loved Kendra, she always felt like the odd one out. She was the child who had been rejected by her own mother.

Because Kendra's family was poor, she drew taunts and slurs from classmates at school. As a result, she began to care about her appearance and went to great lengths to play the part of a popular, normal child. She dreamed of the day when she could leave her history behind and build a life that others would respect.

Years later, as an established professional, Kendra came to counseling complaining about the emptiness of her life. A successful businesswoman and active church member, Kendra knows how to impress others with her credentials and vivacious personality. Yet she still has nights when she sobs into her pillow, asking God, "Why didn't my mother love me?"

Even her closest friends don't know about the inadequacies that have haunted Kendra throughout her life. How can she risk further rejection by admitting the humiliation of her past? Instead of dwelling on these fears and heartaches, Kendra forges ahead in her strengths, the acceptable version of who she has become.

You don't have to have a dark secret or a tragedy in your

past, like Kendra, to feel the sting of shame and a fragile self-image. If you've experienced such rejection, you are simply more in touch with the true human condition. *Regardless of your heritage and history, you were destined to wear a mask since the day of your birth. You entered this world with deep needs that could never be fully met because you were created for a relationship that was severed through sin.* Although God designed you for fellowship with Him, you were born on the Enemy's turf, alienated from the very purpose of your being. You bear the image of a righteous Creator but fail at every level to participate in the fellowship and the glory for which He designed you.

And so, as a young child, you learned to survive by wearing masks. This is the way of the world: You must do something great, be friendly, follow the rules, make others laugh, have a quiver full of children, be extremely talented, be highly educated, or look beautiful in order to be a person of value.

Based on your background, natural talents, and personality, you created a mask that seems to fit you so perfectly that most of the time you aren't even aware of its presence. Seldom, if ever, have you realized how drastically it cripples your fellowship with God or your intimacy with others. Your mask feels as much a part of you as your own skin. It is simply who you've become.

In the 1980s, a film called *The Breakfast Club* captured the attention of pop culture. Although the movie earned an R rating, youth workers within prominent churches and Christian organizations were urged to see it because of its effective portrayal of humanity. The story takes place at a suburban high school on a Saturday during detention. The film brilliantly captures the struggle for identity among five students who serve the daylong detention together. The cheerleader, the jock, the punk, the rebel, and the geek begin the morning at odds and with nothing in common. But as they share throughout the day, they learn how similar they truly are. As the day wears on, they in turn divulge their fears, pain, and feelings of rejection. The rebel tells about his abusive father, and the jock explains his pressure to succeed. They are each fighting for a place in a lonely, callous world. Each has assumed an identity—a mask—for survival.[2]

Perhaps you remember this vivid struggle for identity as a teenager. It was probably during these tumultuous years that you settled on how you would define yourself. Was it based on looks? Boyfriends? Grades? Sports? Parties? Money? Clothes? Talents? Or did you leave high school still lost? Perhaps you defined yourself not by what you could do but by what you couldn't do. Stupid. Ugly. Rejected. Ordinary.

Although you probably no longer feel that raw insecurity of adolescence, the pain and the questions may lurk just below your "mature" adult identity. Adulthood feels more secure only because you've grown more comfortable and confident in your mask.

Nothing holds both the potential to heal us more completely or wound us more deeply than simply being genuine. The hope of healing awakens the deep desire to be fully known and valued. This longing sometimes triumphs over fear and prompts us to take risks, to be vulnerable. But that honesty and nakedness alerts us to real dangers. Only when we're truly ourselves can we be utterly rejected.

All of us have experienced the hurt of sharing too much and having our trust met with betrayal. Yet we also know the loneliness of tucking away secrets and stuffing feelings. Our lives hang in the balance of this choice: to risk being known or to hide behind the safety of a role, a facade, an identity. So goes the struggle of who we are, who we pretend to be, and how we hide. You may hide so well that you aren't even aware of what you're doing. But since the fall of Eve, to be human is to be hiding.

WHAT'S AVAILABLE AT THE COSTUME SHOP

I have heard of your paintings too, well enough;
God has given you one face,
and you make yourselves another.
—WILLIAM SHAKESPEARE, *Hamlet*

Perhaps a quick browse through common masks will help you recognize how deeply entrenched our culture is in this masquerade. Here are several that women hide behind:

- Jamie is protected by her armor of accomplishments, possessions, and power. Her travel schedule, luxury car, Palm Pilot, and never-silent cell phone proclaim her importance. People are impressed when they find out how quickly she has risen in the business world. Few ever think to look behind her success and get to know the real Jamie.

- Kate is the neighborhood's supermom. Kids are always playing at her house. Her minivan sports her children's honor-roll stickers. Kate's schedule is packed with sporting events, Moms In Touch, field trips, homework, cooking, laundry, and cleaning. As long as her children are developing well, Kate is assured that her life is meaningful. What could be more important than building the next generation?

- Shauna hides on her college campus. Gone are her insecure high-school days; she has grown in her confidence. She's earning a 3.6 GPA at a prestigious university and is surrounded by friends and male admirers. Seldom does Shauna give voice to the loneliness of her soul.

- If you have a problem, call Karen. She's the best friend a woman could ever have. Karen never says no and would do anything for someone in need. She lives to be needed. Who she is beyond that, not even Karen knows.

- Vicky is one tough lady. She knows how to get things done, but don't get in her way. Vicky has no qualms about telling you exactly what she thinks. Her motto is "If the truth hurts, too bad." Vicky's aggressive and blunt style serves to keep others at arm's length. No one dares to get close enough to know the real Vicky.

- Are you throwing a party? Kelly should be first on your list. If Kelly can't make it, reschedule, because she's the queen of fun. Always armed with entertaining jokes and stories, Kelly is a blast to be around. She's loud, friendly, and can make even the shyest person feel welcomed. Her charisma and charm will make you forget that although you've known her for years, you still have no idea who she is.

Where do you fit in? How have you crafted your life into an identity? Are you a perfectionist, a peacemaker, a know-it-all, a socialite, a beauty queen, an introvert, or a helpless victim? Do you realize how powerfully your struggle for acceptance and meaning defines you? Your days are packed with work, relationships, duties, and leisure. But to what end?

But wait, you may be thinking. *Maybe what you're talking about is just my personality. How do I know if I'm wearing a mask or if I'm just being myself?*

Heather was always eager to volunteer for projects at church and her children's school. Although her husband sometimes complained that the family was overcommitted, Heather genuinely believed that her service was an expression of her personality rather than a mask. However, as she delved deeper into the issue of self-esteem, she began to realize that being available and helpful were primarily her way of gaining attention and friendship. Her insecurities faded into the background as others applauded her servant heart.

After praying about this for a couple of weeks, Heather decided to "fast" from volunteering for six months. She was amazed at how difficult it was to say no and let other people down. She began to feel useless and doubted her worth in the body of Christ. She wondered if people would still appreciate and value her as a person rather than as someone who could be trusted to complete a task. In the absence of busyness, she discovered how threatening it felt to call a friend just to have coffee with her. Without a mutual project to work on, what would they talk about? How much of herself would she have to reveal?

Like Heather's, your mask likely emanates from your personality traits, strengths, and past experiences. God created you with a unique temperament and approach to the world. Don't confuse that uniqueness with your mask, although they may appear to overlap. A genuine characteristic becomes a mask when you use it to hide or protect yourself rather than to express the real you. Authenticity displays who you truly are while masks manipulate that truth, presenting a more favorable or guarded image.

Your mask is the established pattern for how you interact with the world. It filters how you see yourself, understand others, and solve problems. Most likely this coping style is productive, and even helpful, in many life circumstances. However, the protection your mask provides comes with a steep price, one you may not even know you're paying!

THE GOING PRICE OF A MASK

The price of your mask may be evident only when something goes wrong—a divorce, the loss of your job, the death of a loved one, a financial crisis, the rejection of a close friend, infertility, a threatening illness, a wayward child. When your mask cracks, you realize how empty life feels, how vulnerable your very existence is. Like the man who built his house upon the sand, the waves and the wind erode the foundation of who you are.[3] Only then are you aware of how compromised your life has become by hiding.

Your Mask Prevents You from Experiencing Intimacy with God

Our relationship with God is absolutely dependent upon how we understand ourselves before Him. Throughout Scripture we see examples of people approaching God on their own terms, comfortable in their masks. Perhaps in that moment of awareness, their motives felt pure and their desires seemed to be set on pleasing God. Only as third-person observers can we see how lost they were in their pursuits.

Certainly the most obvious example of these kinds of people were the religious leaders of Jesus' time. The Pharisees had tremendous authority and were treated with great respect in their community. They were the most educated and came from the most prestigious Jewish families. When Jesus came onto the scene, He threatened their masks by inviting sinners and common people to serve God. He exposed the Pharisees' facade of righteousness by pointing out the evil in their hearts. Even under the guise of spiritual leadership, they worshiped their masks rather than recognizing the true God. They chose to kill the source of truth in order to preserve the illusion of their righteousness.

If you're a student of the New Testament, you probably view the Pharisees as the bad guys of the Bible. Less obvious is the fact that we, too, are in danger of sharing their foolishness. The lesson of the Pharisees is that we must never approach God based on our strengths. Our talents, good behavior, knowledge of Scripture, and devotion to God cannot make us worthy in God's eyes. We're strong only when we're willing to be weak. We will embrace God only when we're truly humble, dependent, and childlike before Him. We desperately need Him!

The book of Mark tells of an encounter Jesus had with a rich young ruler. This young man probably was born into the right family, was intelligent, knew the Scriptures, and was a God seeker. He came to Jesus, presented his résumé, and waited to be praised as a worthy disciple. Instead of saying, "Good job,"

Jesus hit this guy square between the eyes: "Go, sell your possessions and give to the poor. . . . Then come, follow me."[4] Intimacy with God is impossible when we approach Him with the facade of a mask.

Notice that Jesus *never* dealt with people based on what they could offer Him. His followers were those who were willing to admit how lost and sick they truly were. Jesus said, "It is not the healthy who need a doctor, but the sick. But go and learn what this means: 'I desire mercy, not sacrifice.' For I have not come to call the righteous, but sinners."[5]

How often do we try to put our best foot forward when approaching God? For example, just think about the Sunday-morning church routine. If you're like me, the "Sunday-morning scramble" probably looks something like this: All morning while getting ready to "worship," you run around the house yelling at your kids and fuming at your husband. Then, because you left 10 minutes late, the car ride is filled with silent tension or flat-out arguing. But as soon as you pull into the parking lot, you remind the kids to paint on their smiling faces and behave in "God's house." Finally, your "happy family" emerges from the car, wearing their Sunday best.

Who are we fooling? Is this how God really wants us to approach worship? God isn't impressed with our talent, beautiful clothes, or well-behaved children. He longs for an honest, intimate relationship with us characterized by dependence on Him.

"Nothing in all creation is hidden from God's sight. Everything is uncovered and laid bare before the eyes of him to whom we must give account. . . . For we do not have a high priest who is unable to sympathize with our weaknesses, but we have one who has been tempted in every way, just as we are—yet was without sin. Let us then approach the throne of grace with confidence, so that we may receive mercy and find grace to help us in our time of need."[6]

Your Mask Prevents You from Pleasing God

How might your life be different if you truly didn't care what other people thought about you; if their opinions, judgments, and gossip held absolutely no weight? Consider John the Baptist, the greatest man to ever live, according to Jesus. John had this freedom. He dressed weird, lived in the desert, and preached a very unpopular message. He was completely unconcerned with the earthly consequences of his spiritual calling.

Although God probably won't call you and me to eat locusts and wear burlap, He does call us to the same kind of devotion to Him. Children of the King should have no regard for the world's opinion of them. In fact, the Bible tells us that because the world hated Jesus, it will hate us as well, so we should expect to be persecuted when we identify with Him.[7]

But that's easier said than done. This world has such a strong hold on us. We long for the approval and praise of others, and our masks are designed to help us gain that approval.

Cindy is a typical Christian wife and mother with a couple of school-aged children. Each day, she spends most of her energy packing lunches, doing laundry, helping with homework, and driving her kids to various sporting activities. Cindy finds great fulfillment in taking care of her husband and children. Her kids are well behaved, get good grades at school, and usually get along with each other. The family lives in a modest suburban house and attends the local community church on Sundays. So what's the problem?

Maybe nothing, maybe everything. We can be going through the motions of what a Christian woman is "supposed to do" without ever pleasing God. Many of the good things we do are ultimately rooted in the safety and accolades of living up to the world's expectations, not in serving the Lord.

Although our masks may be effective and applauded by society, they set our hearts on pleasing people. It's impossible to seek the approval of both God and the world at the same time. *Every thought we have, every word we utter, every motive in our hearts is either intent upon pleasing God or serving our pride.* James 4:4 says it plainly: "Friendship with the world is hatred toward God."

How often I try to walk the line with one foot in this world. I do care what people think! Honestly, I'm often far more concerned with establishing my identity on earth than I am with becoming a disciple of my Savior. Second Chronicles 16:9 says that God searches the earth to find a heart that is fully committed to Him so that He may strengthen it. To be servants of the King, we must renounce our identity in this world. "For am I now trying to win the favor of people, or God? Or am I striving to please people? If I were still trying to please people, I would not be a slave of Christ."[8]

Your Mask Prevents You from Experiencing Intimacy in Relationships

Sue and Jessica are having lunch together, catching up on their families and recent events. After they share about potty-training progress and kindergarten teachers, their conversation drifts toward a mutual friend.

"Have you talked to Emily lately?" Sue asks.

"No," replies Jessica. "We've kind of drifted apart recently. Whenever I'm with her, I feel like she's judging me."

"I feel the same way. She expects everyone else to be able to run a house like she does. I'm glad she homeschools her four children, but some of us have real jobs and need to earn real money."

"I feel really bad for her," Jessica observes. "She alienates everyone. No one really likes to be around her because she's so perfect."

And so their conversation continues. After two hours of heartfelt sharing, the two hug and make plans to meet again in a month.

How typical is this of the relationships women have? Our banter, cloaked in a facade of Christian "love," is often centered on tearing down and outdoing one another. More often than not, our conversations are really two masks talking to each other— proving their worth—rather than two individuals connecting.

This problem isn't limited to girlfriends. Most marriages suffer from the same malady. One spouse is the peacemaker; the other, the achiever. One loves the limelight while the other is content to drift in the shadows.

Often, a couple like Jim and Brenda comes into counseling complaining that they just can't communicate. As I listen to them discuss their problems, I can't help but notice the repetition. Like a warmed-over sitcom, week after week they sit in my office having the same conversation, reading from the same script. Whether Jim and Brenda are talking about the septic tank, Jim Junior's T-ball game, or the family's Christmas plans, they end up at the same place. Jim is always Mr. Fix-It with the quick solution to every problem. Brenda is the nitpicker, ready with 10 reasons why Jim's solution is inadequate. After listening to his wife belittle him, Jim throws up his hands in frustration and exclaims, "I don't care what you do. You take care of it."

The *issues* Jim and Brenda discuss aren't really what impede their intimacy. They can never connect because they don't know how to reach for each other outside of their masks. In the midst of arguing, they never express genuine feelings like "I'm scared," "I'm hurt," or "I'm really sorry." After more than a decade of marriage, neither really knows what exists behind the scripts they so skillfully recite.

Few husbands and wives know how to touch each other's souls. They've settled for a cheap imitation of intimacy, his mask clanging against hers.

Another distressing consequence of a mask is how it distorts parenting. Instead of mirroring God's relationship with His children, parents love and value their kids based on performance or how well they wear a mask. The family superstar is easier to love than the child who struggles with everything. Instead of brotherly love, sibling rivalry flares as children try to win their parents' admiration and attention.

Love and unity are among the most common themes in the New Testament. You wouldn't guess it from looking at the state of the local church or even our own families. Can you imagine if the church really acted as a body? Can you envision having a pure love for every person you know? Jesus said, "A new command I give you: Love one another. As I have loved you, so you must love one another. By this all men will know that you are my disciples, if you love one another."[9]

Honestly, this command seems impossible to live out. How it must sicken the heart of God to see His children playing the Devil's game, calling it Christian love. We will never honor Christ as members of His body until we recognize the lies we believe and ditch the masks.

I was in my mid-20s when I first began to recognize the prominence of my masks. If anyone's family was functional, it was mine. I grew up with two wonderful, loving Christian parents. Yet even in this environment, I felt the desperate need for approval. My universe revolved around my parents' praise. As a young child, I was intent on earning good grades, winning athletic competitions, and behaving perfectly. At the slightest sign of a parent's or teacher's disapproval, I would melt into tears. My parents would reassure me of their love and tell me that winning awards and earning perfect grades made no difference. But I didn't believe them. As one of six children, I wanted to be special. I wanted to make them uniquely proud of me.

This attitude naturally transferred into my relationship with God. If being one of six was difficult, how could I be special as one of billions of God's children? How could I get God's attention? How could I be sure that He loved and noticed me among so many others? I read Paul's words to the Corinthians about running the race to win,[10] and I determined to run the race of life to win—to be the best.

I remember thinking as a young child, *I want to make a mark on this world for God.* If you heard a 10-year-old girl say that, you might be impressed. Well, people were. They applauded and encouraged me to develop my gifts to do just that. Then I got a glimpse of what I was really doing: using standards of spirituality and achievement to establish myself before God. I didn't want to make a mark *for* God. I wanted to make a mark *for myself* before God. There's a profound difference between the two.

As my walk with Christ deepens and the Holy Spirit reveals more of my heart, I'm astounded at the depth of my hiding. I want my children to look good, I want others to admire me and be impressed with what I do, and I rather like hiding behind my busyness and credentials. As I ask God to change my heart, I must be honest about how even the good I do is driven by futile efforts to prove something, to get God's attention, to outdo a colleague, or to control my destiny. My righteousness is truly like "filthy rags."[11]

The struggle doesn't stop even in church. While praising God, I watch the worship leaders, mentally critiquing what they wear and how animated they are as they sing. I look around to see who is in church, which sets off all sorts of selfish and malicious thinking. *God,* I pray, *why can't I even worship You free of this sinful struggle? Why are my thoughts so bound to the survival of ego and human acceptance?* I know I'm sick and that I'm surrounded by sickness. We all look so secure and healthy behind our masks. But we're in need of the Physician who can heal with truth in love.

Nothing hinders my walk with Christ more than this battle that rages within me. Even the things I do for God easily become warped ways of distinguishing myself among other people. When will I want God more than I want what He can do for me?

I believe that no single issue more greatly affects our lives than that of self-esteem. It begins in early childhood and flares violently in adolescence. Although in adulthood the question of self-image appears to be settled, inwardly it rages, hijacking emotions, motives, and beliefs. Our approach to friendship, worship, health, money, work, marriage, parenting, leisure, sexuality, accomplishment, forgiveness, service, witnessing, temptation, and appearance is profoundly affected by our self-esteem. *To the extent that our self-image is skewed by the world, we fail to walk based on God's truth in every aspect of our lives.*

Our Savior died not only to free us from hell but also to liberate us from the bondage that keeps us ineffective on earth. He has invited each of us to uniquely participate in His glory. But Satan has so tied us up in knots about our doubts, shame, insecurity, and pride that we waste our lives playing his irrelevant games.

I pray that through this book, you'll discover how your search for self-esteem can either drive you toward God or away from Him. I pray that God will open your eyes to the ways you hide and will open your heart to His unconditional love and worth. By discovering your destiny and design in Christ, may you learn to walk in the confidence of His truth. I pray that this work will reflect His Word, which is able to transform your thoughts, relationships, and motives.

O Lord, we want the freedom that You died to give us! We want to be free to praise You as Your bride. We want to honor You without a thought of impressing others. We want to fellowship with and serve others without a hint of competition, jealousy, or suspicion. We want to proclaim Your name without the fear of what others will think about us. We want to tell how we were blind but now we see through Your amazing grace.

This is the freedom we seek beyond the masquerade.

Surely you desire truth in the inner parts;
you teach me wisdom in the inmost place.

—Psalm 51:6

Questions for Reflection

1. "To be human is to be hiding." Do you agree with this statement? Why or why not?

2. What masks do you wear? How do your masks overlap with your personality?

3. When do you remember feeling inadequate or unworthy growing up? How might your mask have developed out of that experience?

4. How has wearing a mask interfered with your relationship with God? How has it compromised your significant relationships with others?

2

Seeing Beyond Reality

So we fix our eyes not on what is seen,
but on what is unseen. For what is seen is
temporary, but what is unseen is eternal. . . .
We live by faith, not by sight.
—2 CORINTHIANS 4:18; 5:7

How do you feel after reading the first chapter of this book? Are
you intrigued? Confused? Scared? Challenged? As I teach this
topic in retreats and Bible studies, I find that most people feel a
little desperate at this point. I hear comments like these:

- "Could you just tell me what my mask is and how to get
  rid of it?"
- "I'm not sure I even have a mask."
- "I have so many masks I don't know where to start!"
- "Why do we have to delve into all of this? Can't we just
  serve Jesus without all of this introspection?"

None of us want to hide behind a mask. We would like to believe that we're authentic and genuine in our relationships and service to God. It's tremendously unsettling to think that what we've always believed to be real is perhaps just pretense. As much as we want to grow in our relationship with Christ, we're leery of messing with the foundational security of "being me."

If you have questions, misgivings, and fears, know that you aren't alone. As threatening as the process of "unmasking" before God may seem, trust that the work isn't without great purpose and promise. As full and secure as life may seem behind our masks, we won't be truly free to serve the Lord until He strips them from us. Only then can we begin to see life from the spiritual reality.

Movies such as *The Matrix,* a futuristic action blockbuster from 1999, aren't exactly my cup of tea, but I reluctantly saw it with my husband. The premise of the movie is that Neo, the main character, lives a very normal life until he is kidnapped. He wakes up and realizes that his whole life has been spent in a trance. Computers have taken over the world and manipulated people's brains so they believe they're living normal lives. In reality, the human population is living in a vegetative state, hooked up to a giant computer. Based on brain-wave manipulation, people "dream" about work, relationships, exercise, and every other aspect of life. The computer-generated dream world keeps the human population content and incapable of fighting for their freedom.[1]

Because I'm not a science-fiction buff, this movie would typically be very forgettable for me. However, I still remember it because of its profound correlation with the battle that we fight in the Christian life. C. S. Lewis's book *The Screwtape Letters* has a similar theme. Although we aren't hooked up to a giant computer that controls our brain waves, we are still manipulated into believing a false reality. Satan and his legions don't have to tempt us with the profane as long as they keep us content with the material. To the extent that our existence feels legitimate, there's no need to seek elsewhere for truth. The demons' strategy isn't to blatantly tempt Christians but rather to subtly lure them into the world's thinking.[2]

Our masks are our passports in this world. They make us acceptable and provide opportunities for success, meaning, and comfortable living. Living behind a mask seems so fulfilling. We have good days and bad days. Success, pleasure, and the admiration of others genuinely feel like the real thing—what we were born to strive for. But the Bible tells us there's another reality: "For our struggle is not against flesh and blood, but against the rulers, against the authorities, against the powers of this dark world and against the spiritual forces of evil in the heavenly realms."[3] Whether or not we realize it, that unseen reality is present now in our lives. The Enemy would like nothing better than to keep us too busy and satiated to acknowledge the unseen.

I've spent much of my life entrenched in this world's system of thought. I wake up every day striving for human acceptance and accomplishment. I feel fulfilled when others praise me, and I feel desperate when they reject me. Very seldom do I strive for the things that are unseen and eternal. No one will encourage me for seeking the Lord, nor will they notice when I choose not to gossip or harbor bitterness. I won't receive praise for laying down my prideful thoughts. The material reality (the physical and interpersonal world we live in) seems a lot more rewarding and real! This is exactly why living beyond a mask is so difficult. It means forsaking my place in the only reality I can tangibly know.

We have so much wealth in our culture; there are so many things to keep us busy. We're surrounded by literally hundreds of ways to find our niche and establish our place of importance. Beauty, talent, family, discipline, humor, intellect, education, resourcefulness, and even spirituality are all riches that seem adequate to get us through life. We learn to build confidence and identity in these riches, and for the most part it works. Ironically, the healthier we feel, the sicker we become. As we succeed in the world's economy of self-esteem, we usually drift further and further from a childlike dependence on God.

Striving for meaning and self-worth from a human standpoint is a temporary endeavor. Even if we succeed and the rewards *seem* real, they will vanish when we enter the reality of eternity. The world we "know" is really a manipulation of spiritual brain waves. Although the kudos and successes feel legitimate, they're really meaningless. They serve only to distract us from seeking that which can truly satisfy the soul! This is why Paul tells us to focus on what is unseen rather than what is seen. Even if we're productive and nice people, we become agents of the Enemy when we base our lives on the world's rules. The masks we so depend on keep us rooted in a reality that will one day disappear.

God's Word makes very clear what we often refuse to accept: We cannot play by the world's rules and God's at the same time. We must choose which reality to live in. This one issue, if not clearly understood, makes free men and women unwittingly walk as if they are still slaves of this world.

Satan never presents us with the blatant choice, "You either serve me or God." He's far too clever to openly lay out the truth for us to see. Notice how he tempted Eve in the garden. He played on her desire to be wise and godlike. He planted doubt in her mind about God's goodness and power. He made her believe that she could pursue pride while maintaining her relationship with God. Let's be very clear: *Chasing self-esteem on the world's terms isn't simply self-serving; it is falling right into Satan's hands.*

Throughout the history of humanity, Satan has tried many schemes to distract God's children from spiritual reality. Reading through the Old Testament, we see how Israel stubbornly chose to worship pagan idols instead of depending on God. Bowing down to a clay or wooden statue makes no sense to us, but it was the primary weapon the Enemy used against God's chosen people.

In the New Testament, the early church battled against religious teachers who taught legalism and false doctrine. Paul's letters were filled with sadness as he witnessed young Christians being seduced by false teachers who tickled their ears with myths, and others who preached bondage to the Old Testament Law.

Satan changes his strategies to appeal to each time and culture. Make no mistake—he is still a "roaring lion looking for someone to devour."[4] Read what Jesus said about Satan's schemes: "He was a murderer from the beginning and has not stood in the truth, because there is no truth in him. When he tells a lie, he speaks from his own nature, because he is a liar and the father of liars."[5]

One of the Enemy's primary weapons in our culture is this issue of self-esteem. We may not be tempted to bow down to graven images or to insist that all males be circumcised for salvation, but we're very confused about the golden calf of "self." All our masks are primarily rooted in this confusion. Satan must rejoice as he sees us so content in this world, clinging to our masks for our identity.

Stuck in the Christian Matrix

What about the Christian who really wants to be authentic and doesn't want to play the game of hide-and-seek? How does she even begin to discover the truth about herself? Unfortunately, even with the best intentions, such soul-searching is likely to be extinguished within most Christian circles.

Barb had been part of the same accountability group for years. Twice a month, she and four other women met at a local coffee shop, where they shared life and encouraged one another. With her youngest child going off to college, Barb began asking about the next chapter of her life. She wanted to rekindle the love in her marriage and find a new passion into which she could channel her time. But most of all, she wanted to deepen her relationship with Christ. The looming empty nest, the recent death of her mother, and a few new aches and pains were all reminders that life was ticking away at a rapid pace. As she shared her hunger to know God, her friends nodded respectfully. A few times, Barb explained how God was revealing her strong attachment to the things of this world—how money, comfort, and beauty were the primary pursuits in her life. These comments were invariably dismissed with statements like "You're just too hard on yourself."

We're befuddled with the idea of recognizing and discouraging masks—both ours and others. As attractive as authenticity may sound, we have no idea how to pursue it. Although Christian bookstores are filled with advice on the topics of self-esteem, pride, and authenticity, much of it is contradictory. Some encourage us to embrace the notion of self-love and self-improvement. Others teach that the very idea of knowing yourself or working on self-esteem is of the Devil. So on we trudge, settling for the compromise of life with a mask.

Throughout my years of counseling Christians who battle "self-related" issues, I've noticed two major traps that keep us stuck in the masquerade. Both represent distortions of the truth that the Enemy has effectively used to get us off the scent of authenticity.

Trap No. 1: Christians, Beware of Self!

Recently, a dear Christian woman entered counseling, barely able to make it through the day. For several years Ellen has had all the symptoms of clinical depression, including insomnia, weight gain, crying spells, lack of enjoyment in life, feelings of severe inadequacy, and thoughts of suicide. The first thing Ellen said after sitting down was, "I feel like such a failure for needing to come here. I've tried for many years to pray my way through this. My church teaches that counseling, even for a Christian, is very dangerous and a sign of not depending on God."

Many Christians like Ellen believe that issues related to emotions and self are rooted in material reality. As our relationship with God flourishes, such battles, they believe, should simply fade away. Talking about how we feel and how we struggle is viewed as a sign of spiritual weakness. After all, they assume, true Christians should never have marriage problems, eating disorders, or wayward children. Their trust in God should be enough to obliterate such worldly traps.

Yet, even as we ignore issues of self, they continue to plague the church. Call it what you will, but let's be honest: Who among us isn't faced with real problems rooted in self? Depression, eating disorders, fear of failure, backstabbing, promiscuity, pride, obesity, shame, midlife crisis, pornography, codependency, gossip, addictions, phobias, compulsions, gender confusion, anxiety, panic attacks, sexual abuse, raging anger—these aren't simply psychobabble terms created to drum up business for the local Christian counselor. These are the real-life struggles of the body and bride of Christ. Within every church and every pew, these problems live, sapping the strength and effectiveness of God's children.

When the pretense is dropped, and we're safely within the confines of a therapy room or confessional, we can admit that we're very confused about who we are and who God has created us to be.

Ignoring the problem doesn't make it go away. How many Christians hide their shame and doubt, afraid they won't fit in or they'll be rejected by other Christians? Sexual abuse, promiscuity, divorce, abortion, pornography, thoughts of suicide, daily struggles with sin—we act as if they don't exist among Christians. We have to pretend to be stronger and more "faithful" than we are. In this way, the church actually promotes living the lie of the masquerade.

Like Ellen, Janet was raised in a very conservative church tradition that taught that "self-related" problems were signs of spiritual weakness. Several years ago, she told her pastor that she had been sexually abused as a child. The pastor prayed with her and then advised her not to bring it up again. He was very clear that she shouldn't share her past with her husband because of the damage it might do to their marriage. Janet obediently muzzled her secret and the resulting anger, shame, and questions. She played the part, wore the right clothes, prayed the right prayers, and performed her duties as a wife and mother. Emotionally, Janet was dead—a far cry from the passion and healing Christ died to bring her.

Janet desperately needed her church to be a place where she could be honest and heal through the love of brothers and sisters. Instead, she was told to ignore her insecurity and pain and play the part of a joyful Christian.

Although this approach seems to be spiritually based, it quickly becomes another way of rooting our confidence in material reality. Remember the Pharisees who refused to look at their pain and depravity? Their self-righteousness and spiritual pride were the most dangerous kinds of masks.

Read through the Psalms, Proverbs, and Job. God never asks us to muzzle our feelings and doubts, but to honestly lay our hearts before Him. He was never pleased with those who presented "perfect" sacrifices behind facades of strength. As David wrote, the sacrifices that please Him most are "a broken spirit; a broken and contrite heart."[6]

The answer to the world's egocentric religion of humanism isn't for us to run away from emotional issues. Instead, we must address real-life problems, like depression and inadequacy, from a biblical, eternal perspective.

A huge portion of the work Christ does in our lives is transforming the way we understand self. This transformation is a lifelong process that demands honesty about doubts, pride, shame, guilt, bitterness, and other very messy aspects of being human. Christ's work is done within us and is intricately related to our understanding and experience of self.

Right before my first book, *Finding the Hero in Your Husband*, was published, I was scared to death of the pressure it would place on my marriage. I was 30 and had been married for six years. What did I know about marriage? How would Mike and I stand up under the scrutiny of skeptical readers and the onslaught of Satan's attacks? I was also terrified of becoming proud. How would I react to the possibility of being put on a pedestal in my church and community?

I went to person after person expressing these fears, hoping to find a place to address them. My well-meaning friends and advisors all seemed to say the same thing: "Don't worry. You won't fall into those traps." Yet I knew in my heart how vulnerable I was.

Finally, the Lord brought into my life a friend who affirmed my fears and inadequacy. Instead of reassuring me, she said, "You're right to be afraid. You *are* at great risk. Let's keep talking and praying about this." She provided a safe place for me to take off my "spiritual" mask and tell the truth about the cracks in my heart. Only by addressing my weakness before God and others can I be free from it. Hiding and pretending only enslave me more.

Christ died to free our entire being, not just our actions. To be freed is to be free. *We should never be afraid to ask the deep questions about our worth, our existence, our emotions, and our purpose.* God created us with complex thoughts, personalities, desires, and emotions. He understands how our sinful nature has warped that complexity. His healing truth fills the marrow in our bones only when we're honest enough to lay ourselves before Him, from the inside out.

Trap No. 2: The Bible Is Consistent with Culture

If one camp of Christians denies the importance of self-esteem, the other camp dives in headfirst. When I dropped off my son at the church nursery several weeks ago, the nursery volunteer handed me a sheet of paper titled "25 Ways to Build Your Child's Self-Esteem." As I read through the list, I couldn't help but think that the church has plagiarized the ideas of modern humanism. Change a few words, and this list could have come from any secular self-help book.

Many of our churches approach matters of self by taking worldly thinking and sprinkling "holy water" on it. Start with a self-help concept, take out the naked greed and lust, add a few examples from the Bible, and you have a relevant sermon. This trend started with the sincere desire to reach the world on the world's terms. People who would never come to hear a sermon on the book of Romans will fill the pews to hear how to expand their territory or build their children's self-confidence.

God's truth is relevant to contemporary issues like marriage, relationships, parenting, depression, and work. Helpful teachers draw out the truths of Scripture as they relate to everyday life. However, there is a fine line between using the Bible to support a theory and drawing relevance out of truth.

Take parenting as an example. I was talking to a well-meaning, loving mom the other day who had some concerns about one of her four children. Three of her kids had found their own ways to be special: One was a musician, one a scholar, and one an athlete. This mother's concern was how to help number four find what he could do to be special. I completely understood where this mom was coming from and have had similar thoughts about my own children. After all, who are we if we can't find something we excel at?

But how is this thinking biblical? "Well," you may respond, "Proverbs 22:6 says, 'Train a child in the way he should go, and when he is old he will not turn from it.' I need to find my child's bent and help her be the best she can be."

This message is so dangerously close to the truth that we often can't discern the lie. Yes, God has created each of us with unique strengths, weaknesses, personality, talents, and interests. Good parents help their children develop the gifts God has given for the purpose of glorifying Him and playing a part in the body of Christ. But remember that many of those body parts are very average. What was so impressive about Moses, Andrew, Stephen, Ruth, or Abraham? This world gravitates toward the spectacular, while God exalts faithfulness, servanthood, and humility. Which are we teaching our children to value?

Another distortion is using Scripture to justify the quest for self-love by citing the often repeated command for us to "Love your neighbor as yourself." This principle appears nine times in Scripture throughout both the Old and New Testaments. Even Jesus quoted it.[7] Certainly, it must be important.

Modern Christianity has often interpreted this verse to mean that we have to work on loving ourselves so that we can love others. This is consistent with contemporary psychological teaching: Only when you love yourself can you truly love another person. Although this message sounds good, unfortunately it's a blatant distortion of truth.

The Bible never tells us to love ourselves. In fact, Paul describes a terrible time when "people will be lovers of themselves, lovers of money, boastful, proud, abusive, disobedient to their parents, ungrateful, unholy, without love, unforgiving, slanderous, without self-control, brutal, not lovers of the good, treacherous, rash, conceited, lovers of pleasure rather than lovers of God—having a form of godliness but denying its power."[8] This isn't exactly a glowing endorsement of the self-esteem movement!

When Scripture tells us to love our neighbors as ourselves, the assumption is that love for self is a given. A good analogy might be "Love broccoli as you love ice cream." You certainly don't have to make an effort to enjoy ice cream. The latter represents the standard by which we should strive for the former. Paul says that all humans love themselves and naturally place a high priority on looking out for the interests of self. Self-love is an inherent quality of humanity.[9]

"But there are many people who really hate themselves," you might protest. Suicide, self-mutilating behavior, and derogatory self-talk are good examples of this. Most likely, you've gone through periods in your own life during which you despised your appearance, your personality, your background, or your actions. Don't these experiences refute the concept that self-love is natural?

We're confused because we misunderstand the meaning of love. If loving yourself means positive feelings or appreciation for who you are, then maintaining self-love takes a lot of effort. However, the Bible is referring to a much deeper concept of love: devotion, sacrifice, and commitment regardless of feeling. In this sense, human beings by nature are devoted to their own welfare. *Feelings of inadequacy or self-loathing are simply expressions of self-love.*

I can acutely remember times in high school when I was extremely negative about who I was. I felt fat and had pimples checkering my complexion; I experienced rejection from peers and wondered if anyone outside my family would ever love me. While friends went out on dates, I stayed home wallowing in my misery. Make no mistake: My depression and self-pity were the result of my concern about myself. I didn't shed any tears for classmates who were unattractive or lonely because I wasn't committed to their well-being. My angst came from my devotion to *my* happiness and my inability to gain acceptance from others.

Don't confuse hating your hair, your figure, your learning disability, or your heritage with hating yourself. *Ironically, all feelings of poor self-esteem are born primarily out of love for self. The call to God's children isn't to seek self-love; He calls us to be devoted to others with the same devotion we have to our own personal needs.*

A biblical perspective of self-esteem is built not upon your love for yourself but upon God's love for you. God's love is undeserved, unyielding, and uncompromised. As Jesus said, "I am the way and the truth and the life."[10]

Many well-meaning Christians believe that God wants us to build one another up the way the world suggests. Expressions of inadequacy—"I'm not very smart"—should be met with praise—"Don't say that. You're smarter than I am." Without realizing it, we help one another perfect our masks!

What the Bible says is extreme; it bears no resemblance to the wisdom of Oprah or other talk-show hosts. The power of the gospel is exposing the lies we build our lives upon. Jesus never taught a modified version of culture but instead turned worldly thinking upside down. The weak are strong, the wise are foolish, the righteous are wicked, servants are leaders, the rich are poor, and to find your life, you must lose it. Teaching that God wants us to have beautiful faces, fat bank accounts, flat abs, perfect families, elaborate scrapbooks, fun-filled weekends, and intelligent children is an absolute distortion of the gospel. Yes, God is very concerned about your self-esteem, but not on the world's terms:

> Do not love the world or anything in the world. If anyone loves the world, the love of the Father is not in him. For everything in the world—the cravings of

sinful man, the lust of his eyes and the boasting of
what he has and does—comes not from the Father but
from the world. The world and its desires pass away,
but the man who does the will of God lives forever.[11]

A MESSAGE OF TRUTH

*No one man can, for any considerable time, wear one
face to himself, and another to the multitude, without
finally getting bewildered as to which is the true one.*
—NATHANIEL HAWTHORNE, *The Scarlet Letter*

Although Christians should be aware of and active in self-
esteem issues, our approach should be radically opposed to the
world's. Self-image is a spiritual issue that can be effectively confronted only in the spiritual realm. In fact, a primary theme of
the Bible is a call for us to completely reorient our self-esteem
based on truths that the world rejects. *We falter not because the
quest for self-esteem is humanistic but because we're approaching a
spiritual question with an earthly mind-set.*

No matter how we settle the issue, Satan wins as long as we
stay rooted in the world's thinking! The world believes that we
forge our own worth through self-improvement. The most
important goal is to prove your individual worth. Culturally
speaking, we're all self-made. Even our "spiritual" endeavors are
geared toward the ultimate prize of becoming valuable and worthy people.

The biblical view is dramatically different. Scripture doesn't
ignore issues of self but calls us to address them with the Lord.

Our worth and transformation have nothing to do with our efforts or success at elevating self but occur as we humble ourselves before our Creator. Confession, humility, and healing all require the willingness to examine our hearts, our motives, and our pasts.

Children of God, instead of avoiding self-esteem issues, must approach them based on the truth of Scripture. The ultimate goal isn't self-love but to accept and reflect God's truth. From a worldly perspective, your self-esteem can be good or poor, inferior or inflated, high or low. From a godly perspective, there is only one goal: to understand yourself based on faith and to walk accordingly. Therefore, your self-esteem is either rooted in the truth of God or in the lies of this world. According to which reality do you live?

There once was a man who grew up with every earthly advantage. He was born into a prestigious, wealthy family; attended the finest schools; and garnered the respect of everyone who knew him. This man had energy and enthusiasm for the right things; no one could fault him morally. In fact, after attending seminary, he became a biblical scholar and activist, defending his faith zealously against any threat. Confident in his heritage, righteousness, and accomplishments, he was certainly a person of great value.

One day, this man had an experience that "unplugged the giant computer." By God's grace, his blinders were removed, and he saw the invisible reality of his life. With all of his zeal and good intentions, he had unknowingly become an enemy of God. "Saul, Saul, why do you persecute me?" a voice from heaven asked him.[12] After that encounter with God, Saul (Paul) was never the same. No biblical writer encourages believers to seek transformed thinking more strongly than the apostle Paul because he experienced it personally. Read what he wrote about his altered understanding of self:

> If anyone else thinks he may have confidence in the flesh, I more so: circumcised the eighth day, of the stock of Israel, of the tribe of Benjamin, a Hebrew of the Hebrews; concerning the law, a Pharisee; concerning zeal, persecuting the church; concerning the righteousness which is in the law, blameless.
>
> But what things were gain to me, these I have counted loss for Christ. Yet indeed I also count all things loss for the excellence of the knowledge of Christ Jesus my Lord, for whom I have suffered the loss of all things, and count them as rubbish, that I may gain Christ and be found in Him, not having my own righteousness, which is from the law, but that which is through faith in Christ, the righteousness which is from God by faith.[13]

Prior to his conversion experience, Saul was understandably confident in his pedigree, education, accomplishments, and zeal for God. He was a complete success based on the material reality in which he lived. But after seeing the spiritual reality, he realized how empty his life truly was. The very "masks" he once depended upon, he now saw as rubbish that interfered with his service to Christ.

Throughout the next three chapters, we'll explore three

building blocks of self-esteem: self-worth, self-concept, and self-confidence. God desires that we build our understanding of self in these three areas based on our relationship with Him.

The essential question is, Do you base your self-image on the reality you see, feel, and touch, or do you trust in the truth of God's Word? Living based on truth requires faith, for "without faith it is impossible to please God."[14] You may be amazed at how the world's perspective has dominated your thinking and your actions; but you'll be delighted to experience the genuine freedom our Lord offers His children.

Surely you desire truth in the inner parts;
you teach me wisdom in the inmost place.

—PSALM 51:6

Questions for Reflection

1. Do you believe that Christians have to choose whether to invest in either worldly reality or spiritual reality? Explain.

2. In what ways might your self-esteem be rooted in material reality?

3. What is the danger in ignoring self-esteem issues?

4. How are your insecurities and inadequacies rooted in self-love?

5. "We falter not because the quest for self-esteem is humanistic but because we're approaching a spiritual question with an earthly mind-set." Relate this to the ways you've approached self-esteem issues in the past.

3

Self-Worth:
The Beginning or the End?

Self-worth: the value you give to
your life and achievements
—CAMBRIDGE INTERNATIONAL DICTIONARY OF ENGLISH

Shortly before beginning this book, I turned 35. My way of dealing with this daunting milestone was to evaluate how satisfied I was with my life based on my accomplishments. Here was my frame of mind: *I'm married to a great guy, have three beautiful boys (I've always wanted four boys, and I still have time for another), I have my doctorate degree, I've authored two books, I weigh less than I did in high school, I have a wonderful family and great friends. What else could I possibly want at 35? This is exactly where I pictured myself being.*

Even as I lingered over these reassurances, in my heart I

knew they were from the wrong reality. This is what I was really saying: *Juli, you've made a great life for yourself. Look around. As far as 35-year-olds go, you're doing great. Can you find a life that compares with yours?*

As I evaluated my 35 years, I was really asking, *What have I done or become that distinguishes me from everyone else? How am I special?*

To question our self-worth is as human as breathing. Every day of our lives, we wake up, live through the day, and go to bed ultimately asking one question: *What makes me special?* Sure, we don't voice it audibly. Maybe the question consciously occupies our minds only on those big birthdays. But lurking beneath everything we do, every relationship we have, and every word we say is the compulsive need to become someone who is worthy.

"Am I a person of value?" This is the quintessential question upon which all aspects of self-esteem are built. If you don't believe yourself to be valuable, all of your efforts at bolstering your self-esteem will ultimately fail. No matter how conceited you may act or how many successes you experience, feelings of low self-worth will torment you beneath your facade of confidence.

Shauna is a beautiful woman with a loving husband and a successful career. Because of her friendly and charismatic personality, people are drawn to her. As a young girl, Shauna was sexually abused by her father. Although her mother never talked about the abuse, she knew it was occurring. Her mother openly hated Shauna and blamed her for all the problems in the family. She repeatedly called Shauna a "slut" and a "worthless child."

As an adult, no amount of success or adoration can erase the wounds her mother and father have inflicted. Shauna tries with all her strength to gain the love and admiration of others, but it's never enough to erase the messages of worthlessness that play constantly in her mind.

Jamie has different insecurities about her self-worth. She was born into a wealthy, close-knit family. Her father is a surgeon and a pillar of the community. Wherever Jamie went, doors seemed to open for her because of her father's reputation. When the time came to marry, she had a number of suitors eager to marry a beautiful girl with a fat bank account and a great family name. Many would say that Jamie has good self-worth. After all, what girl wouldn't trade places with her?

However, even though Jamie was born into a stable and "valuable" family, she still struggles with issues of self-worth. Because she must uphold her family reputation, Jamie never leaves the house without a full makeover and designer clothes. She secretly wonders if her Ivy League education and handsome husband have more to do with her father's success than with her own accomplishments.

Each of us has beliefs and "tapes" based on both childhood and adult experiences that seem to determine our self-worth. We spend most of our lives trying to confirm or modify those beliefs.

How do you determine your personal value? What do you base your self-worth upon? Do you take stock of your accomplishments? Do you react to what others say about you? Is it the reflection in the mirror or the numbers on the scale that establish your worth? Whether or not you've consciously settled this question in your mind, your life is built around your conclusions.

As discussed in the previous chapter, we ultimately approach life from one of two perspectives: material reality or spiritual reality. The reality that dominates our being is determined by the answer to this question: "Do I think of myself as a creature or as a creator?" Even if we believe in God and profess that He is Lord, it's easy to live as a creator—the creator of our destinies and our value.

I challenge you, as you read about these two perspectives of human worth, to honestly evaluate how much of your life is spent thinking as the designer and sustainer of your own value. Your struggle for security and self-esteem will continue to pervade all aspects of your life until you're willing to relinquish the role of creator.

As the prophet Jeremiah wrote, "The heart is deceitful above all things and beyond cure. Who can understand it"?[1]

Life as a Creator—An Endless Reality Show

There is no meaning to life except the meaning man
gives to his life by the unfolding of his powers.
—Erich Fromm, renowned humanist and psychologist

I don't like reality-television shows, but one thing can be said of them: They do reveal the reality of the human race. Life is simply one big competition in which there are winners and losers: the valuable and the worthless. Everywhere we go, there's a pecking order of value. Although it's never openly discussed, we have an accepted system of evaluating people in every setting, including churches. Depending on the context, people get votes for education, appearance, personality, position, or wealth.

Why do we endlessly struggle to elevate ourselves above others? *Because apart from the all-knowing, involved Creator, our lives have absolutely no intrinsic worth or purpose.* Without God and His purpose for us, who are we? How can our lives be meaningful? In the quest to answer these questions, we've become enslaved to the world's task of creating an identity. Like it or not, we must play the game of the masquerade to create some semblance of worth or purpose. Let's be honest: This is how we separate the truly esteemed from the ordinary. The rules of this game we play every day of our lives determine our worth in the eyes of the world.

Human Value Is Something to Be Achieved

> *Pride is the recognition of the fact that*
> *you are your own highest value and,*
> *like all of man's values, it has to be earned.*
> —AYN RAND, novelist and philosopher

As a psychologist and a parent, I hear the word *special* endlessly. Our society believes that all people, especially children, need to know how wonderful and important they are. But based on what? Ironically, the very forces that push this "special" theme have absolutely nothing to back it up with! The words are truly meaningless. How can you possibly be special if you're here by chance? How can your life have value if your very existence is random? How, among the billions of people that inhabit the planet, can each individual be important?

Do you know why our culture is so obsessed with self-esteem? Or why the label "special" is the sacred mantra? Because deep down, being our own creators means that we aren't so special after all—that life is nothing more than what we make of it.

The modern self-esteem movement is a farce to cover up the ugly fact that we have no intrinsic value. The same "wise men" who tout self-esteem also believe that people are expendable. Worldly philosophy overtly preaches equality while in actuality it values people differently based on their contributions to society or even more superficial factors. A wealthy, beautiful actress is worshiped, while an unborn baby is thoughtlessly discarded. A brilliant surgeon is considered an asset to the world, while a brain-damaged person is considered a liability. And why shouldn't people be esteemed differently? After all, aren't some of us simply more valuable than others?

According to the reality-game-show of life, each of us begins with a certain amount of self-worth based on random factors such as skin color, nationality, our parents' socioeconomic status, and our inherited gene pool. The ultimate challenge is to discover ways to preserve and increase our personal worth. So, let the games begin!

Other People Get to Determine Our Value

Apart from God, your value today is basically the sum total of what the people in your life think of you. It begins with your parents and then spreads to the opinions of friends, coworkers, and even strangers. What other measure is there? Each of us is in danger of getting "voted off the island" every time we let the team down, make someone mad, or simply don't measure up.

This afternoon I took my minivan to the shop to get it repaired. I had to wait at the dealership for three hours with my two-year-old son, Christian. Yes, there were a few calm moments.

But most of the time, I was on center stage looking like an idiot for the other people in the waiting room.

Christian wanted candy and whined incessantly when I said no. Then Christian decided to throw the magazines off the coffee table onto the floor. I calmly told him to pick them back up. "NO, MOMMY!" he shouted. After turning four shades of red, I scooped up my precious son, took him into the bathroom, and told him quite loudly to sit on the floor for time out. Of course, he screamed like I had hacked off a limb, and then he began kicking the door to the bathroom repeatedly. After about 10 minutes of this, he finally calmed down. You can only imagine the looks I got when we came out of that bathroom! I couldn't tell whether they disapproved of my punishment, thought my kid was a brat, or simply wanted peace and quiet. Whatever the case, I couldn't wait to leave. I asked the mechanic three times, "Is it almost done?"

I cared what these strangers at the car dealership thought of me. Why? Because they were evaluating me. Each one of them drew conclusions about my value based on what they observed. That's a scary thought!

Obviously, the people who actually know me have a more important vote on my value. If my husband or my mother disapproves of me, I'm really a loser. So I avoid conflict, get defensive about my weaknesses, or criticize family members before they can reject me.

"What if they don't like me?" "What if I don't fit in?" "What if I fail?" "What if they find out about my past?" When others have the power to determine your worth, you become extremely vulnerable to their opinions, in both casual and intimate relationships. Your self-worth is absolutely at risk. Therefore, your mask is essential to make sure that others see only what helps you prove your value.

Do you ever wonder why you're so eager to please the people in your life? Why the opinions of your coworkers affect you so much? Are you still longing for that elusive praise from your mother or father? Are you desperate for the adoration of your husband or children? Don't underestimate the power others have to determine your self-worth.

Our Value Constantly Changes

If value is determined by a subjective standard, then your worth is always changing. Your appearance, age, possessions, job, health, and relationships are in a constant state of flux. Just because you were valuable last year doesn't mean that you are today. History is littered with people who were once powerful and famous but who have now been forgotten.

Any human being with a shred of insight will agree that self-worth based on societal standards is like quicksand. People even seem to treat you differently depending on how you are currently "performing." Not only must you wear an acceptable mask; you must also maintain it at all times.

When my first book was published, I couldn't believe what a big deal people thought it was. But the adoration didn't last. Soon I had to give more defining details. How many copies had been sold? Did anyone review my book? If so, what did the reviewer say? Would I get an appearance on Oprah? My self-worth went up and down depending on the answers to these questions.

Not more than six months after my book was published, everyone started asking me, "When are you going to write another one?" One friend even warned me, "You don't want to be a one-book wonder."

I had the same experience after my second book was published. I will never do enough to rest in my worth. I must constantly be striving for new ways to prove my value.

This same dynamic is true no matter what masks you wear. What you accomplished yesterday isn't enough to prove your value today. You must make more friends, never say no to anyone, not look a day over 22, have more children, climb the social or career ladder, and on and on—you fill in the blank. It's enough to fill up your entire life.

And without divine intervention, it will.

When You Win, I Lose

Your true value depends entirely
on what you are compared with.

—BOB WELLS, major-league baseball player

Like a reality show, the world's system of self-worth inevitably leads to fierce competition. If each person is valued based on contribution, then the one contributing the most is the most valuable. A good example of this is the experience of moving on from high school to college.

I distinctly remember my senior year in high school. Because

I went to a small Christian school, I was involved in everything: sports, drama, music, National Honor Society, you name it. My fellow seniors and I felt extremely valuable to the school. In fact, I wondered how the school would survive without us!

Three months after graduation, I found myself at Wheaton College surrounded by two thousand Christian kids who were all smart, talented leaders. How quickly my value evaporated! I was a measly freshman in a crowd that clearly overshadowed any of my high school accomplishments. In reality, neither my abilities nor my personality had changed during those three months. I was the same person, but my value had greatly diminished because of the competition; my contributions were no longer unique.

Human worth is based on a continuum. The only benchmark is the value of other people. You are either more valuable or less valuable than others. Therefore, anyone who has the same personality or strengths as you do is a threat. How can your mask be noticed if it's overshadowed by someone else's? How can you be valuable if your next-door neighbor is more valuable?

Like a reality show, your friend is your friend until she threatens your chances of winning. With this way of thinking, how can we possibly hope for the success of others? Their value inherently diminishes ours.

Forging our own personal value is the backdrop behind practically everything we do—it's all consuming. To be free from masks, inferiority, and insecurity is life changing! Yet this freedom can be ours only as we switch from seeing ourselves as the *creators of value* to the *created with value*.

LIFE AS A CREATURE—A TRUTH TO BE ACCEPTED AND REALIZED

Know that the LORD Himself is God;
it is He who has made us, and not we ourselves;
we are His people and the sheep of His pasture.
—PSALM 100:3, NASB

I don't believe I have ever in my life truly comprehended the depths of my creatureness. Up to this point, I've never been completely at the end of my rope, faced with my absolute dependence on God.

Even if you've had that kind of experience, you probably don't live with it daily. From a material perspective, there are many ways in which you are independent. You probably have the resources to buy food, get a job, make new friends, and generally enjoy life.

In this affluent secular culture, it's very difficult to live as the dependent creatures we are. However, as we yearn to be free from the games that dominate our lives, if we truly want to be free from the masks we wear, we must be willing to embrace the truth that we are nothing more than creatures designed for the purposes of Someone beyond ourselves. After all, how can something that is created possibly have worth outside of its Creator?

Yesterday was my husband's birthday. As the years we share together have accumulated, I've learned that the card I give him is often more valuable than the gift. The paper and the ink are worthless. Even the letters and the words I write are nothing in and of themselves. But they become extremely valuable to the extent that they express my thoughts and feelings to Mike. The carefully chosen card and thoughtfully written words have great meaning because they represent me. Only because they reflect a truth greater than their substance are they valuable.

The same is true of any artist. The paint, the canvas, and the clay are nothing. They take on life and value only as they reflect the intent and heart of the craftsperson.

These examples explain why our worth is so intertwined with God's image. Our bodies are composed of material substances that, apart from life, are worthless. *What makes us priceless is the meaning God breathed into us. Rather than creating our own feelings of self-worth, we find our true value only as we look to the purposes of our Designer.*

God Has Already Determined Your Value

You created my inmost being; you knit
me together in my mother's womb. I praise you
because I am fearfully and wonderfully made;
your works are wonderful, I know that full well.
—PSALM 139:13–14

According to Scripture, it's impossible to achieve self-worth because you already have it. You have great value whether you ever achieve or accomplish anything. There's nothing you can do to add to or take away from your value as a person.

Your value is ultimately based on two facts: *First, you were made in the image of God.* The writer of Genesis recorded that God created the earth and the surrounding universe. Then He filled the earth with animals—reptiles, fish, and every other moving creature. God was pleased with His work but had one final objective: to create the human race. Of all the wonderful and glorious things created, only humans were created in God's image.

You've probably heard the words the *image of God* many times, but don't look past them. They hold a profound message about your worth. Only humans have the potential to rule over creation, only humans can choose right from wrong, and only humans will live forever! *Your worth has nothing to do with what comes out of you but depends instead upon what was put into you.* You were fearfully and wonderfully made. Nothing can change that!

Every embryo, infant, child, teenager, adult, and elderly person has great value. The rich, the poor, the handicapped, the healthy, the mute, the mentally retarded, the beautiful, and the homely all possess the distinction of humanity, the crowning jewel of God's creation.

Not only do you share the image of God with other people; God created you uniquely in His image. He knit you together in such a way that you individually reflect His likeness. You are designed to bring God glory in a way that no other human can duplicate exactly.

Second, you're valuable because God loves you. As if it weren't enough to create humans to innately reflect His glory, our Creator does the unthinkable: He loves us. "Jesus loves me this I know..." Do you really know what it means to be loved by God?

So much of what we experience as "self-worth" is based on who loves us. Can you remember the girl in high school who was chosen to date the football star? She held her head a little higher walking down the hall because everyone knew an important person "loved" her.

When others treat us with affection and care, we feel valuable. When they reject us, we're plagued by a deep sense of inadequacy and worthlessness. If we're so affected by the love of other people, how must the love of God transform our worth? Scripture is full of reminders of that love:

> This is love: not that we loved God, but that he loved us and sent his Son as an atoning sacrifice for our sins.[2]

> And I pray that you . . . may have power, together with all the saints, to grasp how wide and long and high and deep is the love of Christ, and to know this love that surpasses knowledge.[3]

> Give thanks to the LORD, for he is good; his love endures forever.[4]

You've done nothing to earn God's love, but He loves you. With all of creation and every circumstance in your life, He woos you. Because you're worth so much to Him, He sent His Son to be ridiculed, tortured, and murdered so that your relationship with Him could be restored. Knowing this, what could possibly add to or take away from your value?

Your Value Doesn't Change

Probably the biggest difference you'll ever experience between material and spiritual reality is stability. I don't know about you, but my self-worth is all over the place when I let the world dominate my thoughts. One day my husband and I are getting along, my kids are behaving, my friends are all nice to me, and I feel on top of the world. A week later, the septic tank backs up, I get in a fight with my sister, my kids get a stomach virus, and I feel like a loser.

The same is even true with my attempts to please God. There are weeks when I go through serious self-doubt. I wonder if my life makes any difference, I question my abilities, and I despair over my impure heart. Then I get encouragement from someone who has been helped by something I've said or written. I'm ecstatic. I can't wait to get out there and earn more kudos!

That's the way of the world. You're either better than the crowd or worse than the crowd. You're either superior or inferior. On you go, vacillating between pride and inadequacy.

In an interview with Oprah Winfrey, comedian Jay Leno said seriously, "I think high self-esteem is overrated. A little low self-esteem is actually quite good. . . . Maybe you're not the best, so you should work a little harder."[5] Most Christians probably agree with Jay. We think the best place to be on the spectrum of self-esteem is near the middle. That way we avoid both snobtown and loserville. But nothing could be further from the truth. As long as we rely on what other people think about us, even in spiritual environments, we'll be like the double-minded man, unstable in all our ways.[6] How absurd it must seem to God when His creatures look to one another to determine their value!

God calls His children to absolutely reject the world's standards of worth. Feelings of both pride and inferiority are lies because our worth has nothing to do with other people. Instead, we should value ourselves and others based on unchangeable spiritual truths.

All humans are both made by God and loved by Him.

Nobody is more valuable than anyone else. We all derive our worth solely from reflecting the unfathomable glory of our Creator, and that never changes!

Your Value Is Meaningless Unless It Is Realized

In spite of the truths you read in the previous sections, there are some verses in the Bible that might make you question the stability of your worth:

> Is Gilead wicked?
>> Its people are worthless![7]

> And throw that worthless servant outside, into the darkness, where there will be weeping and gnashing of teeth.[8]

> All have turned away,
>> they have together become worthless;
> there is no one who does good,
>> not even one.[9]

> How the precious sons of Zion,
>> once worth their weight in gold,
> are now considered as pots of clay,
>> the work of a potter's hands![10]

The critical message of these verses is that it isn't enough to believe that God created you with worth. Your extraordinary value must also be realized.

In the book *The Man in the Iron Mask*, the queen of France

gave birth to a son, Louis XIV. Only a few people knew that she also gave birth to another boy, Phillipe, only minutes later. To protect Louis' place on the throne, Phillipe was stashed away with a family in a poor town, where he grew up as a pauper, unaware of his true identity. As a young adult, Louis learned about his identical twin and rival to the throne. He kidnapped his brother, sealed an iron mask on his head to forever hide his likeness, and threw him in prison.[11]

What good was Phillipe rotting away in a remote prison cell? Of what value was his royal lineage if neither he nor anyone else recognized it?

God created you to be His daughter, His princess. Because of the iron mask of sin, you've been banished to a filthy cell, completely divorced from your royal destiny. Although your value hasn't diminished, it's meaningless as long as you remain masked and separated from the King and Lover of your soul.

This is the state of humanity and why we feel the compulsive need to chase after the elusive promise of self-esteem. Although we were created to reflect glory and righteousness, we live in the gutter of sin and depravity. Jesus died to free us from that iron mask. Without His sacrifice, we couldn't possibly be free from the chains of worthlessness.

HOW WE REALIZE OUR VALUE

The most important way we realize our value is through *relationship*. Think of the two undeniable facts that should be the foundation of your value: You were created uniquely in God's image, and He loves you. Unfortunately, those facts are often nothing more than pleasant, lofty thoughts. You cannot possibly reflect God's image or truly know His love without being connected to Him.

God has a different relationship with His children than He does with those who are separated from Him. In fact, the Bible says that until we place our trust in Christ, we're actually children of Satan, lost in the lies of the masquerade.[12] But because of Jesus, every person can choose to be in God's family.

A person who has accepted Christ's gift of salvation is no more valuable than a person who hasn't. However, one is free to become the person God created her to be, while the other remains tragically enslaved to vanity. Without a relationship with God through Christ, your value will never be realized!

This is an important truth that the parable of the prodigal son brings home. You can read the story in Luke 15:11–32, but here's a brief summary of the plot: The younger of two sons went to his father and asked for his inheritance early. The father gave him his share of the family's wealth, and the son went off to a distant country and blew everything in wild and profligate living. Only after he'd spent his last coin and was feeding pigs for a living did he recognize his foolishness and return home to his father.

Now, even though the young man had the privilege and identity of sonship, he refused the relationship. His birthright and value were thrown away because he rejected his father's name. Only when the son accepted his father's love, embracing his heritage, could his true value be realized.

Unfortunately, many of us in God's family still think and act according to the world's vanity. We ignore or trivialize our heritage in Christ. The church is just as filled with masks as the world because we fail to embrace the value God has placed upon His children.

The second way we realize our value is through *purpose* (not to be confused with accomplishment!). Once we've established a relationship with God through trusting in Christ's blood, we're His children. Even though that relationship should free us to fulfill God's purpose for our lives, we often wander aimlessly.

A few years ago, a friend convinced me of the nutritional value of juicing. Excited about the vitamins and nourishment it would provide for me and my kids, I went to the health-food store and paid two hundred dollars for a juicer—a great investment in health. For about a month, I juiced all the time: carrots, celery, watermelon, peaches. If it had juice, it got juiced! Then the juicing began to take its toll. It was really messy and took a lot of time. Plus, the kids were less enthusiastic about their carrot and pear juice than I'd hoped they would be. All this to say that the juicer has now been collecting dust in my pantry for more than two-and-a-half years.

The juicer was expensive. To someone who likes to juice and is willing to take the time to use a juicer, it's a valuable tool. But right now, it's worthless to me. I'd be happy to get $10 for it at a garage sale.

You and I are just like the juicer. We are inherently valuable and made to do a very specific job. But when we sit on the shelf, collecting dust, our purpose and therefore our value is thwarted! This is what Jesus meant when He said, "You are the salt of the earth. But if the salt loses its saltiness, how can it be made salty again? It is no longer good for anything, except to be thrown out and trampled by men."[13]

God created you and freed you to be His servant. You are special because He formed you to praise and serve Him uniquely. This purpose is the fulfillment of your worth. When you walk with God and follow His calling in your life, you'll experience the value you've always been searching for!

How you answer the question of your worth unquestionably determines the course of your life. From material reality, the *goal* of life is to establish and maintain personal value. But rather than being the goal, in spiritual reality, your unchanging value is the *foundation* of your life. The following diagram illustrates how unstable our worth can be when not based on a solid foundation of faith.

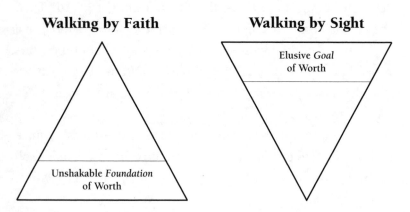

Walking by Faith

Walking by Sight

Elusive *Goal*
of Worth

Unshakable *Foundation*
of Worth

WHY DO WE LIVE AS THOUGH WE'RE NOT FREE?

[The Pharisees] loved praise from men more than praise from God.
—JOHN 12:43

As I write about these truths, the two realities are so clear to me. I sincerely want to be free—to base my worth 100 percent on the truths of God. So why do I find myself entrenched in the world's thinking?

When we live according to the world's reality, our struggle is to achieve value. Living according to spiritual reality presents a different struggle: faith. You may intellectually agree with everything you just read about your worth. But can you believe it in your heart? Are you free from all endeavors to prove your worth?

While the world offers tangible feedback on self-worth, God's truth requires believing in something beyond what we can see. The applause, the praise, the jeers, and the rejections are so easy to believe. But the truth of God's unchanging promises concerning our value doesn't seem possible. How can my value not change when I gain 50 pounds, lose my temper, fail at my job, or apply for welfare? Such a concept is beyond my understanding.

The reason we're so bound to the world's thinking, even as God's children, is that we don't know God. To be God's creation and to bear His image is nothing more than a nice thought without an intimate knowledge of who He is. We walk around with a vague, fuzzy idea of self-worth that gets completely drowned out by what the world says about our value.

As a child and young adult, I thought of disciplines like reading the Bible and praying as duties. I had to do them because they were required. How childish and shallow! How can my self-image ever be transformed without knowing God? How can I live out His purpose for my life without hearing His voice?

The only way for us to truly live according to TRUTH is to walk with God more than we walk with the world. The messages of our culture scream to us about our worth. The feelings are so real and convincing. But God's truth is like a whisper. He's waiting for us to be quiet enough to hear Him.

When my heart really worships God, when I sing about His greatness from the depth of my being, I get a glimpse of who He made me to be. Nothing else matters in the moment. Both accomplishments and failures fade away, and I become engrossed in being a creature rather than a creator.

To switch this perspective of human value is absolutely life changing. Here's why. From a human perspective, proving your value is life's ultimate goal. Your relationships, work, and play all revolve around this motive. Everything you do ultimately has its roots in your becoming a person of worth.

God, however, offers you unchanging worth from the very moment of your existence. Can you imagine how free you would be without the need to achieve, impress, and compete? The value God places on your life is a solid foundation of your being rather than an elusive goal!

To realize this great gift, you must be willing to surrender your status as a creator. The "freedom" of being the creator of your worth means slavery to a mask. You'll spend your entire life chasing a goal you can never accomplish. To be truly free of the compulsive quest for self-worth, you must bend a knee and realize that your very existence is irrevocably intertwined with the purposes of your Creator.

But, as Henri Nouwen writes,

There are many other voices, voices that are loud, full of promises and very seductive. These voices say, "Go out and prove that you are worth something." . . . They are always there and, always, they reach into those inner places where I question my own goodness and doubt my self-worth. They suggest that I am not going to be loved without my having earned it through determined efforts and hard work. . . . As long as I remain in touch with the voice that calls me the Beloved, these questions and counsels are quite harmless.[14]

Surely you desire truth in the inner parts;
you teach me wisdom in the inmost place.

—PSALM 51:6

Questions for Reflection

1. Think of the communities you live in (church, school, work, neighborhood, town or city, etc.). Are people valued differently in each community? Do you value people differently? Based on what?

2. Why does the world's approach to self-worth ultimately result in competition and jealousy?

3. Why is viewing yourself as a creature so important to understanding your self-worth?

4. What keeps you from realizing your worth in Christ?

5. How does your relationship with God affect your worth?

4

Self-Concept: True Lies

Self-concept: the mental image one has of oneself
—MERRIAM-WEBSTER'S ONLINE DICTIONARY

Theologian and author Thomas Merton made this poignant observation about authenticity:

> God leaves us free to be whatever we like. We can be ourselves or not, as we please. We are at liberty to be real, or to be unreal. We may be true or false, the choice is ours. We may wear now one mask and now another, and never, if we so desire, appear with our own true face. . . .
>
> To work out our own identity in God, which the Bible calls, "working out our salvation," is a labor that requires sacrifice and anguish, risk and many tears. . . . We do not know clearly beforehand what the result of this work will be, the secret of my full identity is hidden in Him.[1]

Have you ever kicked around the idea of going to counseling or actually gotten up the nerve to go? If so, you know the fear that accompanies the desire for help. You have to tell the counselor your secrets and give her access to the real you—the one behind the mask.

Because of the potential vulnerability, few people ever muster up the courage to make an appointment. Harvard University recently published research about what happens to those brave souls who actually begin counseling. About half of them drop out! Sure, maybe some didn't like their counselors, but the most common reasons cited are unwillingness to open up and disagreement about what the problem is.[2] The counseling room is both frightening and exciting. It's one of the only places in our culture where absolute honesty is expected and tolerated. Clients are wasting their time and money as long as they keep their masks on.

When I was a freshman in college, I took advantage of the campus counseling center and made an appointment with a counselor. During our first session, I talked about some issues I had with my family. The counselor then made some observations about my relationship with my parents that I didn't want to hear. I never went back.

As a counselor, I've met with people who had the same reaction I had to counseling during my college days. They're either unwilling or unable to look at the truth about themselves. They come to counseling hoping I'll reinforce the lies they believe. "The problem is: My husband. My boss. My mother. My children. My past." The moment I turn the spotlight on how they can change, they bail. This is perhaps the greatest lesson I've learned as a psychologist: We're willing to suffer incredible pain for the sake of preserving our illusions.

Mental and spiritual health can be measured by how accurately you see yourself and allow others to see you. Imagine three circles: one representing how God sees you; the second, how you see yourself; and the third, how others see you. You have a healthy and true self-concept when those three circles overlap evenly (see the following diagram).

In a perfect world, others would know only a part of you, but all of what they know would overlap with what's true about you. You would understand quite a bit about yourself, and all your self-knowledge would coincide with God's complete knowledge of you. Everything you know about yourself would be accurate and based on truth. Likewise, all that others see about you would be genuine, even if they couldn't see the whole picture.

Unfortunately, we live in a world that doesn't encourage or even tolerate such honesty. Our self-concepts are pretty warped. Only some of what we accept about ourselves is actually true. Even further from the truth is the "me" we allow others to see. To the extent that these three circles don't overlap, we're living the masquerade, projecting and even believing lies about ourselves. The diagram on page 74 illustrates the difference between a healthy integrated self-concept and an unhealthy fragmented self-concept.

If you accept this illustration of a healthy self-concept versus an unhealthy one, then you'll agree that we live in an extremely dysfunctional culture that readily exchanges truth for lies. More than 90 percent of Americans claim to believe in God, but the great majority of them have no interest in accepting what He says about them. Rather than believe unflattering

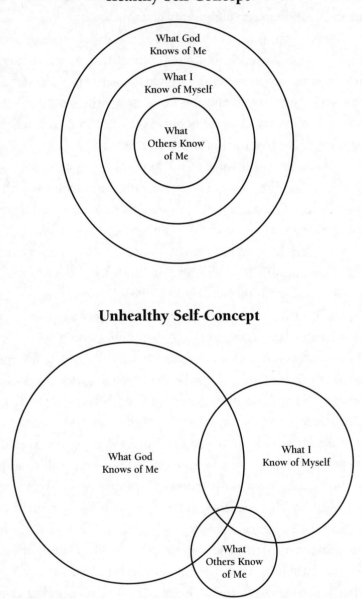

biblical truths, our society combats "negative" self-concept by preaching affirmations.

Affirmations are positive statements about yourself that psychologists may tell you to repeat aloud several times a day to convince yourself that you really are a good person. Here are a few common affirmations that are supposed to boost your self-concept:

- "I'm a strong and powerful person."
- "I can handle whatever comes along."
- "Even if I make mistakes, I always have good intentions."
- "I am entitled to happiness."
- "I have the answers within myself to all my needs."
- "I'm a beautiful person."
- "I'm the master of my existence."

The self-help section of your local bookstore is filled with messages like these. The problem with these nice thoughts is that they aren't true. The goal of such affirmations is actually to deceive yourself! True self-help begins with honesty. As Winston Churchill said, "Man occasionally stumbles over the truth, but usually manages to pick himself up, walk over or around it, and carry on."

In the last chapter, I wrote about self-worth as either the foundation or the goal of our lives. As long as our worth is in question, it's incredibly threatening to admit our ugliness. Because our value depends on being productive and desirable, any flaw is inherently a liability. We have to hide the unacceptable and somehow convince ourselves of a flat-out lie. The diagram on page 76 illustrates how chasing after self-worth only leads to an inflated self-concept rather than an accurate self-concept.

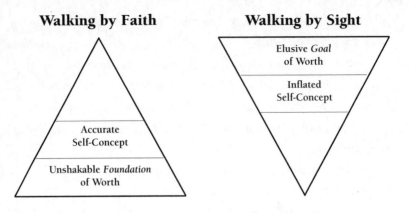

Walking by Faith

Accurate
Self-Concept

Unshakable *Foundation*
of Worth

Walking by Sight

Elusive *Goal*
of Worth

Inflated
Self-Concept

A SERIES OF UNFORTUNATE TRUTHS

The greatest test of where your value rests is determining whether your self-concept is accurate. When others have the power to determine your value or when you must convince yourself that you're a worthy person, the truth is naturally a threat. Is your security in Christ so great that you can accept who you really are? When you read the Bible, are you transformed by truth? When you're ready to take off your mask, you'll invariably discover five key truths about yourself.

Truth No. 1: You Are Sinful (Really, Really Sinful)

> *There is no one righteous, not even one; there is no one*
> *who understands, no one who seeks God. All have*
> *turned away, they have together become worthless;*
> *there is no one who does good, not even one.*
> —ROMANS 3:10–12

If you could follow me around for a day, you would probably conclude that I'm a pretty good person. You might hear me utter a bit of gossip, tell a "little white lie," or mildly lose my temper, but that's about it. There are times when I believe that I basically have the "sin" thing mastered. But let me tell you, nothing could be further from the truth!

Barely a day goes by that I don't hear someone describe someone else as a "good person." This is absolutely the opposite of what the Bible says, yet we so often believe it. We fall for this lie because we have a superficial definition of sin. We consider an "evil" or "immoral" person someone who consistently does something clearly wrong, like adultery, murder, or stealing. As long as we avoid the Seven Deadly Sins, we're "good" people.

The Pharisees thought they were good people too. After all, they followed the Law perfectly. But Jesus responded to them by saying this: "You are like whitewashed tombs, which look beautiful on the outside but on the inside are full of dead men's bones and everything unclean. In the same way, on the outside you appear to people as righteous but on the inside you are full of hypocrisy and wickedness."[3]

Jesus consistently taught that outward obedience or sacrifice is empty. Our hearts are incurably wicked, and every good thing we do originates from selfish motives. Even the apostle Paul wrote that his heart constantly wrestled between the desire to serve God and the pull to satisfy his sin nature.

Let's return to the parable of the prodigal son. If you remember, the young man rebelled against his father and left his home to sleep around, get drunk, and squander his inheritance. Truly he was a sinner needing his father's forgiveness. However, one of the characters we tend to skip over in the story is the older son, the prodigal's brother. This guy lived faithfully with his father and never sinfully rebelled, but he was resentful and jealous when his dad made such a fuss over the return of his prodigal brother.

Which of the brothers was more in need of forgiveness? One brother's sins were external, while the other's were hidden. As Henri Nouwen meditated on the older brother in this parable, he wrote this about his own sinfulness:

> I saw my jealousy, my anger, my touchiness, doggedness and sullenness, and most of all, my subtle self-righteousness. I saw how much of a complainer I was and how much of my thinking and feeling was ridden with resentments. . . . I was the elder son for sure, but just as lost as his younger brother, even though I had stayed "home" all my life.[4]

Whether your sin hangs on your sleeve for the world to see or is tucked away in your thoughts and attitudes makes no difference. Do you understand the extent of your sinfulness? Have you ever peered into the selfishness, pride, and rebellion of your heart? *Putting an end to sin is impossible through determination or self-control. You can never will yourself to stop sinning. Only when you realize this are you ready to fall into the arms of your Father.*

Truth No. 2: You Are Not in Control

> *The heart of man plans his way,*
> *but the LORD establishes his steps.*
> —PROVERBS 16:9, ESV

One of the most effective tools in counseling is to give clients a sense of control. For example, a woman enters counseling because she's tired of being walked on. She's a doormat in her marriage, her kids boss her around, and she can't say no to anyone. The goal of counseling is to teach her to be more assertive, more in *control* of herself within relationships.

Another woman was in a terrible car accident. After weeks in the hospital and painful rehabilitation, she's terrified of driving. Anytime she tries to get behind the wheel, panic ensues. She can't breathe, she trembles, and she feels as if she's going to have a heart attack. To ever drive again, she must gain *control* of her fear.

Control effectively provides the illusion of safety. And, yes, it is an illusion. There are far more things you can't control in life than things you can. You can't control your husband, your kids, your boss, or the weather. You can't even control whether you take another breath.

Sure, we make choices every day that drastically affect our lives. The main message of Proverbs is to make those choices wisely. Likewise, the New Testament implores us to live a life that's pleasing to God. But in spite of all the decisions we make, we still lack control.

Last year, Mike and I took our kids to an amusement park. One of their favorite rides was the old-fashioned cars. I went on the ride with my six-year-old, who was thrilled to be driving Mom around for a change. Although my son really believed that he was controlling the car, there was a metal bumper between the tires to keep the car on the road. *Clang! Clang! Clang!* My neck was sore from all the times the car was corrected by that guide rail!

This is exactly how we live. We can change direction, slow

down, or speed up, but we can never go beyond what God wills or allows in our lives. Although there are many aspects of our lives that we can govern, far too often we overestimate our control.

Andrea believed that if she followed God and made good choices in her life, blessings would follow. She was prayerful about all her major decisions and was a wonderful friend, mother, wife, and daughter. Although she was a health nut, running four days a week and eating organic fruits and veggies, she was diagnosed with fatal colon cancer at the age of 32! Within a year, she was dead, leaving behind her husband and three children.

No one can explain what happened to Andrea. Healthy, nice young people are supposed to live long, happy lives. Children are supposed to grow up with their mother's love.

In Western culture, Andrea is the exception rather than the rule. But throughout the world, many people realize how little control they have. Every day, wars, earthquakes, tsunamis, mudslides, and diseases take the lives of those they know. As Solomon noted, the good and bad alike are victims of hardship and tragedy.[5]

Although God is good, life is not. There's nothing you can do to avoid the inevitable pain, sorrow, and death of your existence. Don't fall prey to the false doctrine that those who love God have happy, pain-free lives. You can't control your destiny by putting more money into the offering plate or being kind to a stranger. Ironically, the only thing we can control is what controls us. Read what the apostle Paul had to say on this matter:

Don't you know that when you offer yourselves to someone
to obey him as slaves, you are slaves to the one whom you
obey—whether you are slaves to sin, which leads to death,
or to obedience, which leads to righteousness? . . . You
have been set free from sin and have become slaves to
righteousness.[6]

So why is the illusion of control so attractive? Why do you
feel better when you think you're in control? There's no way to
be at peace with your lack of control until you truly understand
God's power and love. It's the difference between trusting "fate"
and trusting the Creator and Savior of the universe. Without
God, feeling in control is necessary for survival because you've
become the god who must hold everything together.

Truth No. 3: The World Doesn't Revolve Around You

> You turn men back to dust, saying, "Return to dust,
> O sons of men." For a thousand years in your sight are
> like a day that has just gone by, or like a watch in the
> night. You sweep men away in the sleep of death; they are
> like the new grass of the morning—though in the morning
> it springs up new, by evening it is dry and withered.
> —PSALM 90:3–6

Developmental psychologists will tell you that it's normal for
people to be completely egocentric before the age of four and
again during adolescence. Throughout these periods of "normal
development," humans can see only what they want and need.

The goal of parents of either toddlers or adolescents is to teach them sensitivity and an awareness of others so they will learn that the world consists of more than what they as individuals want, feel, need, or think.

If we take an honest look at our culture, most of us have never made it out of adolescence emotionally. In my heart of hearts, the world still revolves around *me*—*my* children, *my* marriage, *my* house, *my* money, *my* church, *my* country, and *my* health.

This is a blind spot for the American church. Just as it is with worldly thinking, the emphasis in many churches is on *me*—*my* salvation, *my* spiritual journey, and *my* fulfillment. Spiritual conferences and retreats unceasingly offer opportunities to feed *me* and draw *me* closer to God. God exists to serve *my* purposes. He must answer *my* prayers and give *me* the peace and joy *I* want.

Ironically, Jesus said that those who really know Him are servants who focus on others, not on themselves! There are two ways to look at life: from within our own skin and from outside ourselves. Both perspectives are necessary. We're not to neglect what God is doing inside us, but it's only a small part of the whole picture.

We see this contrast in the life of David. The Psalms and 2 Samuel give very different perspectives on the same events. In 2 Samuel, we read about the facts of David's life and the role he played in the nation of Israel. His part was a significant one in God's story, but it was only a part. His life served a purpose far beyond him. The Psalms, on the other hand, give us a glimpse of what it was like to be in David's skin. He couldn't see the big picture of why Saul tried to kill him or why his son Absalom led a revolt against him. He just cried out to God in his anguish and fear.

A healthy self-concept is one in which you see yourself as a small part of God's great plan. You play a part in the story, but you are not the story! Think of heaven. Imagine the wonderful paradox of praising God with millions of others, yet in that same moment knowing God more intimately than ever.

As much as this book is about self-esteem, remember that who you are can never be found without getting out of yourself! As a believer, you're a part of the body of Christ. No matter what part you play, your life is useless if you aren't connected to the rest of the body. As Paul wrote to the Corinthian believers, "If one part [of the body] suffers, every part suffers with it; if one part is honored, every part rejoices with it. Now you are the body of Christ, and each one of you is a part of it."[7]

Some of the most valuable lessons I learned as a child came from the direct result of having five siblings, all close in age. No matter how much my parents may have loved me, their lives couldn't revolve around me. I was a valuable contribution to something larger than myself. I learned how to listen to seven other people each evening at dinner. I learned to honor my siblings when they excelled, and I cried with them when they failed. By necessity, we all had to work and communicate for our family to function. Each child was uniquely valued not only as an individual but also as a part of the whole.

As a member of the body of Christ, you possess both strengths and weaknesses that have an impact on the rest of the body. The eye can see, but it can't speak. The foot is useful but not exactly beautiful. The liver is vital even though we can't see it in action. To understand who God made you, you must remember that you're a part of something larger than yourself.

Truth No. 4: All Your Strengths Are 100 Percent from God

"For who makes you different from anyone else? What do you have that you did not receive? And if you did receive it, why do you boast as though you did not?"[8] I read this verse anytime I speak in public. Unless I really flop, at least a few people are bound to come up to me and say, "You're a great speaker!" or "You're so wise for your age." My flesh wants to linger in this praise. On the way home, I replay the words of praise in my mind, congratulating myself. How absurd! If I can speak or write or counsel, it's only because God has given me these gifts for His glory and to encourage the body of Christ.

Self-help strategies encourage us to focus on our talents and strengths, as if they somehow make us better people. Focusing on our strengths never improves our self-concept; it only inflates it. The truth is that we can do absolutely nothing of significance apart from God. We deserve no glory and no praise. All of that belongs to God. He alone is responsible for anything of value within us.

What strengths do any of us have that didn't come from God? Both natural talents (intelligence, musical ability, athleticism, creativity, beauty) and our spiritual abilities (discernment, teaching, hospitality, mercy) come directly from Him. So why do we take what God has given and use it to compare ourselves with others? Even within the church, we honor and value people based on their strengths, with no regard for the Giver of those gifts. Henri Nouwen wrote:

I am constantly surprised at how I keep taking the gifts God has given me—my health, my intellectual and emotional gifts—and keep using them to impress people, receive affirmation and praise and compete for rewards instead of developing them for the glory of God.[9]

It's only healthy to think about our abilities and talents within the context of who gave them to us and why. We may work hard, practicing and perfecting our abilities. Yet even so, we must remember that God's intention is that all of our strengths glorify Him and serve His purposes. His desire is that the concert pianist who practices hours each day does so not for her own glory but as an instrument of praise. God has given each of us specific talents and spiritual gifts, not for our own edification, but for the church's: "Now to each one the manifestation of the Spirit is given for the common good."[10]

There's a wonderful sense of purpose, not pride, when you discover how God has uniquely gifted you to serve Him. Your strengths are an integral part of who you are. Rejoice when friends and fellow Christians point out your gifts and talents. Marvel in the amazing truth that God has equipped you to do a part of His work. You are necessary and valued within the family of God, but only because of Him!

Truth No. 5: Your Weaknesses Are Greater
Than Your Strengths
"But he said to me, 'My grace is sufficient for you, for my power is made perfect in weakness.' Therefore I will boast all the more gladly about my weaknesses, so that Christ's power may rest on

me."[11] This is one of those verses that doesn't seem to make much practical sense. When was the last time you boasted about or celebrated your weaknesses? When have you felt blessed by your scars, your pain, and your limitations?

Countless times, I've sat across the counseling room from women who share grisly stories of the past—stories about being abused by fathers, grandfathers, brothers, and pastors. A common feeling these broken women express is, "I feel tainted; I can never be whole."

In our society, such weakness is likely to be despised and perhaps pitied. The only hope and advice the world can offer is, "Move on and make a new life for yourself; put the past behind you and create a new image."

The message of Scripture is profoundly different. Rather than telling us to hide the stain of the past, God promises that He can turn *any* weakness and hardship into great strength. Only when we're weak and hurting do we truly seek Him. In our strength, we have no need for God.

The Bible says that God chose the weak, the foolish, the lowly, and the despised things of the world to shame the strong, the wise, and the esteemed so that no one can boast.[12] When you succeed because of your strength, you receive glory. When you succeed in spite of your weakness, you give God glory.

The Bible is filled with weak men and women whose lives reflected the uncompromised strength of God. God chose a guy with a speech impediment (Moses) to preach to Pharaoh. He appointed a coward (Gideon) with an army of three hundred men to defeat the mighty Midianite army. God picked a barren 90-year-old woman (Sarah) to carry a promised child; and a man who was so afraid of being killed that he lied repeatedly (Abraham) to be the father of our faith. Jesus picked a woman from whom He had cast out seven spirits (Mary Magdalene) to be one of His close friends, and a stubborn blowhard (Peter) to be the foundation of His church.

Gonxha Agnes was a homely girl. Because her father died when she was young, Gonxha grew up in a poor family. There was nothing remarkable about her, no salient strengths esteemed by the world. When she was 18, she left home to pursue God's call on her life as a missionary. Throughout her humble life of service, God's strength and love miraculously flowed through the woman who became known to the world as Mother Teresa. Regardless of their religious views, people called her an "angel of mercy." Mother Teresa lived the power of God's love not because of any human strength but because of her dependence on her Savior. She was an instrument of a love greater than herself.

How are you coping with your pain and weaknesses? Do you hide them behind a mask of artificial strength? If you want to be used by God, surrender your limitations to Him. Your weakness is far more valuable to Him than your strength, for it causes you to be dependent on His great power. As a friend once reminded me, "You need to take yourself less seriously and God more seriously."

These five truths are contrary to *everything* the world tells you about yourself. What society calls a "healthy" self-concept is really an inflated and entirely false view of who you are.

Have you ever gone through an entire day without looking in the mirror? In your mind's eye, your hair, makeup, and clothes look perfect. At the end of the day, you peer into the bathroom mirror to a comical sight. To your surprise, your hair is sticking up, your mascara is smeared under your eyes, and there's lipstick on your teeth. Suddenly, it dawns on you that you've gone through at least part of the day looking somewhat like a circus clown!

If we strive for a "positive" self-concept, we may feel and believe affirmations that are completely untrue. We're called to look into the mirror of God's Word and take to heart the truth it reflects—even if that truth is painful.

What the Bible says about us is certainly not complimentary. Some people fear that meditating on these awful truths will inevitably lead to depression and inadequacy. After all, how can focusing on our sin and weakness bolster how we feel about ourselves?

The purpose of a biblical self-concept is not to make us feel good about ourselves but to let us experience the reality of God's goodness to us! We can never know the greatness of God's love until we accept our utter unloveliness—"While we were still sinners, Christ died for us."[13] All that is good and loving and righteous is God. Only when we stop believing that we innately possess these qualities can we seek the true Source of them.

Do you understand why realizing your self-worth in Christ is so critical to an honest self-concept? You have nothing to prove and nothing to fear. No sin, weakness, or limitation can possibly detract from God's love or the value He has placed on you. There's so much freedom in accepting who you are. No hiding, no pretending, no masks. Just a broken person ready and willing to be used by God. Larry Crabb said it beautifully: "When we see our depravity, it doesn't lead to self-hatred but to freedom."[14]

Surely you desire truth in the inner parts;
you teach me wisdom in the inmost place.

—Psalm 51:6

Questions for Reflection

1. What is a "healthy" self-concept?

2. Draw the three circles illustrated in this chapter (representing God's knowledge of you, your self-knowledge, and what others know about you) as they relate to your self-concept. To what extent do they overlap?

3. What are some examples of the cultural message that "the world revolves around me"? How has it affected the church? In what ways have you been tempted to buy into this lie?

4. How could your weaknesses be more valuable to God than your strengths?

5. Which of the five truths discussed in this chapter is the most difficult for you to accept? How might shifting your focus of self-worth (as discussed in chapter 3) help you in this area?

5

Self-Confidence:
Just the Tip of the Iceberg

*Self-confidence: behaving calmly because you have
no doubts about your ability or knowledge*
—CAMBRIDGE INTERNATIONAL DICTIONARY OF ENGLISH

When I was 13, my family moved from Ohio to South Florida. I was a shy, awkward adolescent in the middle of a drastic change. I had lived in the same house and attended the same school and church my whole life. As the fifth out of six kids, I was immediately recognized almost everywhere I went. No one knew my first name, but they all knew where I belonged. A few times a day, I would inevitably hear, "There goes another little Rybka."

After the move, I knew no one and no one knew me. I was just another pimply face in the crowd. One of my first ventures to meet new friends in Florida was our local church youth group. I remember my first visit like it was yesterday. We were playing a game with newspapers strewn all over the floor, and the goal of the game was to quickly find and pick up whatever section of the paper you were assigned. As I reached down to pick up my designated section, I heard a dreadful sound: *r-r-r-i-i-i-i-p-p-p*. My pants had split right up the back. Whatever shred of self-confidence I had started the evening with was now completely gone. I wanted to shrivel up in the corner of the room and cry.

Have you ever felt like that? Exposed? Totally unprepared and ill-equipped for the demands of the situation? Think back to that time, and you'll be reminded how vital confidence is to your functioning.

We thrive on confidence. What would you rather play—a game you're the best at, or one you've never played before? Where would you rather be—in a room full of people among whom you're the leader, or with a group of people who are your superiors? Where would you rather work—in a job that capitalizes on your natural abilities, or in one you have no knowledge of or experience doing? The world simply looks like a better place when we feel confident.

Self-confidence is the belief that we can affect or control our environment in some way, that we can make a difference. A person without confidence inevitably lives on the sidelines, a victim of circumstances. Self-confidence begins with the ability to change yourself. Have you ever set a goal you didn't believe you could achieve? That goal was worthless. Henry Ford said, "Whether you believe you can do a thing or not, you are right."

Confidence is a vital factor in both the cultural and spiritual perspectives of self-esteem. However, the Bible and the world differ drastically on where confidence comes from, what it's placed in, and how it's established.

SELF-CONFIDENCE: A PAPER TIGER

If you have no confidence in self, you are twice defeated in the race of life. With confidence, you have won even before you have started.
—MARCUS GARVEY, journalist and civil-rights leader

Material reality places substantial importance on confidence. Perhaps no trait is viewed as more valuable. It's considered the golden road to both respect and success. Without confidence in yourself, how can others trust your abilities or your character? Your self-doubts are a glaring weakness, which the world will quickly and efficiently exploit.

Think of the enormous success of motivational speakers like Tony Robbins, Victor Hansen, and Jack Canfield. The heart of their message is that you must believe in yourself. If you believe in your own ability, you can accomplish anything. If you're a middle manager making fifty thousand dollars a year, you can be a millionaire if only you can see yourself as one! As Norman Vincent Peale wrote, "Believe in yourself! Have faith in your abilities! Without a humble but reasonable confidence in your own powers you cannot be successful or happy." At all costs, find ways to build your confidence. Take the credit for successes and blame others for your failures. Attempt only those things you're sure to succeed at. Practice, practice, practice until you can't possibly fail.

One of the major goals of psychology related to self-esteem is changing thoughts. The reason the affirmations listed in the last chapter are so critical is because they bolster self-confidence. If you step out of the house believing that you're a beautiful and powerful person, people will treat you like one. You create your own reality, and people respond to it.

Confidence is the absolute foundation of self-esteem from a material perspective. If you don't believe in yourself, you can't possibly become a person of value. In the world's paradigm, your self-confidence is the ground-level tool upon which you build your self-esteem. Only when you have great confidence in yourself can you have a positive self-concept. And only when you're working from a positive self-concept can you behave in such a way that people will deem you worthy.

Chloe is the pride and joy of her parents. After three boys, they finally had a daughter. Practically from the time Chloe could walk, she took dance, gymnastics, and music lessons. Day after day, she heard from her brothers and parents, "Chloe, you're so smart. You're so cute. You're so talented." She believed them.

Chloe entered the world of school with great confidence and carried herself with the self-assurance that made her a natural leader. Unlike her awkward classmates, Chloe sailed through adolescence. Class president, captain of the cheerleading squad, honor-roll student.

Failure and rejection have been largely foreign to Chloe. Built on a foundation of great confidence, she believes that she can do just about anything. Her natural talent and charm shine as she lives like the capable, intelligent, successful, beautiful person she believes herself to be. The people around her respond with adoration, envy, and applause. Chloe is truly a valuable person to those who know her.

According to the world's paradigm, Chloe is the picture of how self-esteem should work. Her experience is what the great majority of well-meaning parents want for their kids. The key to a happy life and self-respect, they believe, must be confidence.

So what's wrong with Chloe?

It Just Ain't So!

The problem with basing self-worth on confidence is that confidence is empty. As self-assured as Chloe may seem, a day will come when she'll doubt herself. When she gets to college, perhaps the guy she likes will reject or ignore her, or she'll find that college is harder than high school, and she can't pull the highest grades in all her classes. When she looks for her first job, maybe the competition will be so fierce she won't get the job she wants and will have to settle for something less prestigious. When she marries, perhaps her husband won't treat her with the deference everyone else does. How will she recover when she realizes that she's not so special, that she, too, can experience rejection and failure?

A recent trend in education has been fueled by the self-esteem movement in our culture. "Affective education" programs develop curricula, objectives, and classroom procedures based on making kids feel better about themselves. According to the educators who adopt this philosophy, children are crushed by rejection and failure. Mistakes marked in red or a letter grade below a B leaves a psychological scar that can permanently impair a child's confidence, and therefore his or her self-esteem. So children never have their mistakes corrected, nor are they given grades. Schools are filled with posters that declare such affirmations as "You're a winner." Self-confidence has become far more important than actual learning.

The research on this educational strategy shows the absurdity of this thinking. Instilling empty self-confidence is an abysmal failure on all levels: behavioral change, academic achievement, and future academic and vocational success. In fact, there's often an inverse relationship between a child's actual academic accomplishment and how confident he or she feels.[1]

Telling a kid she's smart when she hasn't learned a lick of math actually sets her up for failure rather than success. Telling a boy that he's a brilliant musician because he played "Mary Had a Little Lamb" will eventually destroy his confidence when he learns that the affirmations were hollow. The fact is, even if Ashley doesn't receive the D she deserves in the fourth grade, someday her boss won't be so sensitive. In reality, life is filled with setbacks, rejection, and struggles. True confidence will develop as Ashley learns to accept and work through the truth. It's far better to grow through an area of weakness than to pretend it doesn't exist.

Confidence is only as valid as what it's placed in. Although positive thinking may work some of the time, it will inevitably run up against reality. Motivational seminars and books encourage you to place your confidence in something that isn't worthy of it. They might as well be begging you to row across the Atlantic in a canoe. No matter how hard you believe, it just won't get you there. Based on what God says about humanity, there's not that much to place confidence in!

Nothing compromises true self-confidence more than pretending to be someone you're not. What you're taught to believe about yourself often dramatically conflicts with reality. That sets up the need to act as though you're smarter, more beautiful, more successful, more talented, and more charming than you actually are—hence the mask.

Controlling, demanding, manipulative, and arrogant behavior is almost always a display of outward confidence to protect genuine insecurity. As confident as we may appear wearing a mask, insecurity rages inwardly. In fact, the more we cling to the confidence of our masks, the further we drift from the stability of knowing who we are.

Self-Confidence Is One-Dimensional

The world's version of self-confidence is always limited. There's no such thing as an all-around self-confident person because no one can be good at everything. People gravitate toward their natural strengths so that they appear and feel more confident most of the time.

Masks are born out of our compulsive need to have self-confidence. We stumble upon an area or action in which we have success. That success leads to a sliver of confidence. In the attempt to repeat the success and bolster our confidence, we build our lives around people and activities that give us a natural advantage. As time goes on, we become more and more comfortable and confident in our chosen masks.

If you pride yourself on beauty, you may gravitate toward people and places that focus on outward appearance. You might be more comfortable at a Mary Kay party than playing flag football. On the other hand, if your confidence is based on your intellect, you likely thrive in settings like book clubs or Bible studies. Perhaps you avoid purely social gatherings at all costs. (Guilty as charged!)

True confidence, however, is invested not in a skill or a job description but in the unshakable foundation of who you are.

Over the past 20 years, Carol was a devoted stay-at-home mom. She never missed a school activity and prepared dinner almost every night for her family. She made her daughters' prom dresses and had kids over to her house almost every weekend.

After her youngest child graduated from high school last year, Carol slid into a deep depression. The one thing she had poured her life into was gone. As we talked, Carol shared how shocked she was to realize how much of her self-esteem was wrapped up in being a mom. How can she be a worthwhile person now that her kids no longer need her?

Who is the successful businesswoman when she retires? Who is the star athlete when she loses? Who is the wife when she is divorced or widowed? Who is the daughter when her parents die? Who is the beauty queen when she ages? Who is the scholar when she starts to slide into dementia? Who is the socialite when her money and friends are gone?

That big birthday, a job loss, a divorce, a major illness, the death of a loved one, wrinkles, physical limitations—when these realities hit, self-confidence is destroyed or severely shaken. Woe to the person who has nothing beneath the mask in which to place her confidence!

GOD-CONFIDENCE: A ROARING LION

But blessed is the man who trusts in the LORD,
whose confidence is in him.
—JEREMIAH 17:7

One of a Christian's fundamental life tasks is to have an impact on her world. Through her love, purity, generosity, and generally good behavior, the world should know that she's different. Matthew 5:16 says, "Let your light shine before men, that they may see your good deeds and praise your Father in heaven."

Making an impact on the world in this way requires confidence. A leader of any type must have clear direction, convictions, and the confidence to live them out. Jesus' apostles changed the world. They were so confident in the message they proclaimed that most of them died for it.

A hallmark of security in Christ is confidence. Whereas self-confidence is the foundation of material self-esteem, true confidence is the outgrowth of biblically based self-esteem (as illustrated in the diagram on page 100). It's not something you have to work on; it's the inevitable by-product of understanding yourself in the light of who God is and who He made you to be.

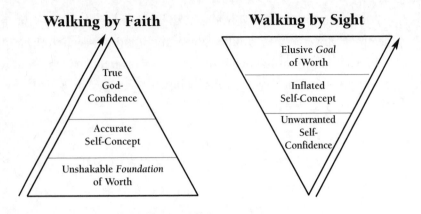

Walking by Faith

- True God-Confidence
- Accurate Self-Concept
- Unshakable *Foundation* of Worth

Walking by Sight

- Elusive *Goal* of Worth
- Inflated Self-Concept
- Unwarranted Self-Confidence

The fundamental distinction between the two worldviews is this: Confidence in the material realm must be placed in yourself; confidence from a biblical perspective is always placed in God. Everything we are and everything we're able to do is rooted in our Creator and Savior.

The Confidence to Be Yourself

> *"If you hold to my teaching, you are really*
> *my disciples. Then you will know the truth,*
> *and the truth will set you free."*
> —JOHN 8:31–32

A few years ago, a friend of mine made a statement about self-esteem that really puzzled me. He said, "I don't know what the big deal is about self-esteem. If you tell the truth all the time, you'll have good self-esteem."

My gut reaction to his observation was, "How simplistic!" I've worked for months with clients on self-esteem issues. If it were as easy as telling the truth, psychologists would be extinct! However, there is profound meaning in his solution: The truth *can* set us free.

Have you ever told a lie and then spent the next several days or weeks trying to cover it up? When I was a freshman in college and away from home for the first time, my mom had strict rules about staying on campus. Feeling the need to test my wings, I hitched a ride with a roommate to Ohio during a long weekend. I had a good friend who lived there whom I hadn't seen in a year. I knew my mom would never go for it, so I just did it. I made up a story about studying all weekend and thought that would be the end of it.

Unfortunately, my brother and several other family members lived in Ohio at the time, and I was paranoid about bumping into one of them. The weekend went without incident until the last day, when I ran into old family friends. Not wanting to admit my deceit, I never asked them to keep my visit quiet.

On the way back to Chicago, I was tied up in knots and terrified that my parents would find out. For the next few weeks, I just waited for the other shoe to drop. When I talked to family members on the phone, I fished around to see if the cat was out of the bag. The anxiety took such a toll on me that I actually became physically ill. My folks never found out about the trip to Ohio, but I ended up having to come home from school for two weeks with mono!

Lying takes a *lot* of work. When we live with a mask, we're essentially living a lie. We waste enormous time and energy keeping up the deception, hoping that no one will discover the truth about who we really are, our sins, our limitations, and our inadequacies. Imagine the freedom of not having to pretend anymore.

How did you feel while reading the truth about yourself in the last two chapters? Were you encouraged? Depressed? Was it hard to see your weaknesses and sin nature for what they really are? As difficult as it is to face your ugliness, great confidence will be the result when you do.

God wants to use us just the way we are. He works through our weaknesses and fallenness. *The power to change the world comes not from our strength but from Christ shining through our brokenness. Those secrets you try so hard to hide can become sources of great confidence when you see the power of Christ working through them.*

As a college student I volunteered at a local crisis-pregnancy center. The director of the ministry, Vicky, was a dynamic woman who took me under her wing. I learned from watching her counseling women in crisis pregnancies, speaking to audiences about abstinence, and helping others recover from the trauma of past abortions. Vicky readily shared the source of her calling— her own abortion years before.

Vicky is a beautiful and talented woman. She could easily achieve success in business, fashion, or many other venues without sharing the most traumatic and vulnerable event of her life. Yet she chooses to let God minister through her out of the pain of her past. Her confidence comes not from her natural ability but from God's work in her life.

My friend was right. Self-esteem does come through accepting the truth, telling the truth, and living the truth. But this is easier said than done.

The Confidence to Do Something

Jesus looked at them and said,
"With man this is impossible, but not with God;
all things are possible with God."
—MARK 10:27

Several months ago, our pastor asked a question from the pulpit that really challenged me: "When was the last time you attempted something that, without God, would surely fail?" His question struck a cord with me for two reasons: first, because I hate to fail; and second, because I hate to be dependent. Both are direct threats to my self-confidence. So why would I intentionally seek out opportunities that involve the risk of both failure and dependence?

Witnessing to a coworker; giving a large portion of income to charity; quitting a job because of ethical compromises; adopting a child; admitting an addiction; starting a neighborhood Bible study; staying in an unhappy marriage; caring for an aging parent; loving the unlovely—each of these represents an insurmountable task without the power of Christ.

Think of Abraham raising a knife to sacrifice his son, Isaac; Hannah bringing Samuel to serve in the temple when he was only three years old; Noah taking decades to build an ark; Moses demanding the release of the Israelites from the mighty Pharaoh; Stephen preaching Christ's love before a throng poised to stone him; David standing before Goliath with a slingshot; Paul preaching to the prison guards; Rahab hiding the Israelite spies from her countrymen. Because of their great confidence in God, each of these servants was used mightily for His purposes!

My pastor wasn't just suggesting that we do something for the sake of risk. Living the Christian life isn't a game of truth or dare; risk for the sake of risk is foolishness. However, each of us has areas in our lives in which we don't fully serve Christ because of the risk involved. Where is He calling you that you're unwilling to go? In what area of your life is God demanding that you place complete confidence in Him?

Watchman Nee said, "God never asks us to do anything that we can do. He asks us to live a life that we can never live and do a work that we can never do. Oh, how Christians need to see this truth!"[2]

The Confidence to Do Nothing

> *Be still, and know that I am God; I will be exalted*
> *among the nations, I will be exalted in the earth.*
> —PSALM 46:10

As difficult as it is to step out in faith and follow God, it can be even more difficult to do nothing. "What did you do today?" It's a harmless question we ask one another all the time. Our days are filled with doing: getting, making, fixing, finding, achieving. It feels good to be moving, doing something. Likewise, it can be incredibly threatening to our sense of self to do nothing. We usually don't even realize how addicted we are to doing until we try to be still.

A few months ago a good friend asked me if I was interested in going on an overnight silent retreat. At the retreat, participants were allowed to bring only a Bible, a pen, and a journal (plus clothes and toiletries). I really wanted to go—to be quiet before the Lord. Although that time frame didn't work out, I was able to have my own "silent retreat" a few weeks later while I was recovering from a medical procedure. But after about four hours of praying, reading Scripture, and praising God, I was clueless! I didn't know what else to do. I was amazed at how low my tolerance for "not doing" was. I realized that I didn't know how to "be" with God without doing something.

How can we know God and develop our confidence in Him if we never stop doing? Think of the great heroes of the Bible and all the time they spent waiting. David wandered around for years avoiding Saul. The time between his anointing as king and his crowning was about 25 years. How about Joseph? As a young man, he had dreams of being great for God. But his brothers sold him into slavery in Egypt, where he served Potiphar faithfully, only to be falsely accused and sent to the slammer. Then he sat in a prison for at least two years doing nothing. God told Abraham that he would be the father of a great nation. Yet there were many decades of waiting and wondering between God's promise and the birth of Isaac. Before His public ministry began, Jesus went into the wilderness to be with His Father for 40 days.

What was God doing in the hearts of these men during all this waiting?

Do you have enough confidence in God that you're willing to stop? To wait? To be still? To be quiet and just listen for Him? I love what Henry Blackaby imagines that God wants to say to us: "Don't just do something. Stand there!"[3]

The "waiting" periods of our lives often are not just spent waiting. They're usually filled with trials, doubts, despair, and voices that taunt us. Few, while waiting, ever believe that God will once again find a use for them. As a "waiting" client expressed, "I feel like God has put me on the shelf to collect dust. What if He forgets that I'm there?"

Indeed, being still calls for great God-confidence.

False Confidence in God?

Trust in him at all times, O people; pour out your
hearts to him, for God is our refuge.
—Psalm 62:8

The Bible is a dynamic motivational book. There are many verses that do an excellent job of bolstering our confidence. These inspiring verses are perhaps some of the most well-known in Scripture:

I can do everything through him who gives me strength.[4]

We know that in all things God works for the good of
those who love him, who have been called according to
his purpose.[5]

If we know that he hears us—whatever we ask—we know
that we have what we asked of him.[6]

In all these things we are more than conquerors through
him who loved us.[7]

God is with you in everything you do.[8]

These verses all promise God's presence and help in times of trouble. Often, we live just like the world does until a crisis or challenge hits. Then we turn to God's Word for encouragement. It doesn't take long to find the verses that make us feel better and instill confidence.

Some people call this "name-it-and-claim-it spirituality." If we only quote the correct biblical affirmations, what they promise will be ours. No! No! No! Read each of these verses again *in context,* and you'll see that what they promise isn't for everyone. God's promises are for those who love Him and seek Him with all of their hearts. God isn't a vending machine that will dole out assurance to whoever asks. Confidence in God *first* requires that we abandon confidence in ourselves!

Having built our self-esteem on the worldly paradigm, we cannot "borrow" the great confidence that comes from God. *The promises of the Bible are profound, but each has significant qualifications. We must be very careful not to use them as Band-Aids on the corpse of self-love.* Biblical affirmations to instill confidence can be just as empty and deceptive as the world's affirmations if we claim them apart from depending fully on our Savior.

To lean into the amazing assurance that God offers His children, we must be willing to relinquish all that keeps us confident in self: accomplishments, wisdom, family, personality, appearance, relationships, possessions, education, status. We must remember that trusting in God comes at a price: "If anyone would come after me, he must deny himself and take up his cross and follow me."[9]

Most American Christians have this mind-set: "God helps those who help themselves." We place all confidence in our own resources and abilities. Confidence in God is reserved only for emergencies.

Whenever the Bible speaks about confidence, it always gives us a choice: Either put your confidence in God or in something other than God. You can't have it both ways. You either trust yourself and the things of this world or you trust God.

Israel's first king, Saul, is an excellent example of how we often try to serve the Lord. Saul consistently mixed in a little bit of God with his own wisdom and confidence. As a result, he was never secure in the power of God in his life. When Saul first became king, he hid to avoid his responsibility.[10] By the end of his reign, he was insane with jealousy toward David, who would eventually replace him on the throne.

The turning point of Saul's reign was the battle against the Philistines in Gilgal.[11] His men were terrified when they saw the enemy advancing. Saul knew that he wasn't supposed to fight until the prophet Samuel arrived to present offerings to God. He waited seven days and then panicked. Instead of waiting longer for Samuel, Saul prepared the offerings himself. Here's what the Lord said to Saul through Samuel once the prophet arrived:

> "You acted foolishly," Samuel said. "You have not kept the command the Lord your God gave you; if you had, he would have established your kingdom over Israel for all time. But now your kingdom will not endure; the Lord has sought out a man after his own heart and appointed him leader of his people, because you have not kept the Lord's command.[12]

Think of the irony of Saul's actions. He sacrificed, asking for God's blessing, while acting in direct disobedience. He acted as if God's plan for him was flawed. Saul went through the motions of trusting God while ultimately acting on self-confidence.

How often do we behave just like Saul? We pick and choose when we'll trust the Lord. God is a jealous God. He won't be a "safety net" for His children. Jesus said to the rich young ruler, "Sell your possessions and give to the poor . . . Then come, follow me."[13] Jesus was telling the young man to get rid of what he put his confidence in. Only then would he be free to trust in God. No halfway!

God's will for us is that we wholly trust in Him for everything. He matures us and disciplines us by taking away the things in which we place confidence. In our culture, we talk about God's blessings of wealth and prosperity. But those very "blessings" often keep us from placing our confidence in Him. Who needs God when you have a steady job, healthy children, plentiful food, a comfortable home, good friends, and three cars?

This is a huge reason why we're so stuck in the world's view of self-esteem. As long as we build from a foundation of what we can do, what we have, and who we know, we'll never experience the freedom of trusting Christ for our worth and confidence.

This is what Jesus meant when He said, "It is easier for a camel to go through the eye of a needle than for a rich man to enter the kingdom of God."[14] In our riches, how can we seek God? In our comfort and wealth, how can we know the joy of placing our confidence only in Him! Consider the words of Watchman Nee, a great Christian leader in communist China:

God desires to bring us to the point where our natural strength is touched and fundamentally weakened, so that we dare no longer trust ourselves. With an abundance of strength we are useless to God. With no strength at all, we can hold onto Him. And with His strength flowing through us, "We are more than conquerors."[15]

Oh, what riches and blessings—not of this world—the Lord has in store for those who wholeheartedly put their confidence in Him! May you and I be found among His faithful!

Surely you desire truth in the inner parts;
you teach me wisdom in the inmost place.

—Psalm 51:6

Questions for Reflection

1. Think of a time in your life when your self-confidence was shot. What impact did it have on your self-worth?

2. What areas of your life do you tend to put confidence in? How stable is your confidence in these areas?

3. What is something God may be calling you to do that requires absolute confidence in Him?

4. Read 1 Samuel 13. Think of an example from your life when you behaved like Saul. How would the situation have been different if your confidence had been 100 percent in God?

5. What's the most difficult thing about placing all of your confidence in God? Why is it impossible from the world's "psychological pyramid" on page 100?

6

Wholeness Requires Brokenness

Several months ago, I was diagnosed with an autoimmune disorder called Graves' disease. Simply put, my thyroid gland was overactive. Although I was always jittery and could rarely relax enough to get more than a few hours of sleep, I didn't mind many of the symptoms of the disease, such as more energy and increased metabolism. In fact, much of this book was written in the middle of the night while the house was still and I was wide awake.

About seven weeks ago, I underwent a radioactive treatment that essentially destroyed my thyroid gland. Right now, I'm experiencing the fallout from life without a thyroid. Eventually, the doctor will put me on synthetic thyroid hormone, and I'll be "normal"—whatever that is. But first, they will let me bottom out.

All that to say that over the past few weeks, my self-esteem has taken a big hit. In spite of careful eating and regular exercise,

I've gained about 15 pounds (weight has always been a hot button for me). My face and eyes are very swollen. I can barely muster the motivation and energy to get the laundry done, and I feel close to what I had previously experienced with postpartum depression. My moods are all over the place: One minute I feel like crying; the next minute I want to punch something. I'm sure it doesn't help that it's the beginning of January; here in Cleveland, we never see the sun between December 15 and March 1.

Yesterday at work, more than a handful of people made comments like, "Are you okay?" "You look like you got hit by a truck." "What happened to your face?" They were too polite to comment on my tighter-than-normal clothes, probably assuming the weight gain was the result of too many Christmas cookies. After work, when I ran some errands, I was acutely aware of avoiding eye contact with strangers. Even dressed professionally and made up, I felt deformed and ugly. I haven't faced this kind of insecurity since junior high!

Why am I surprised that this is happening while I'm writing a book about self-esteem? I asked myself. Of course, the message of this book kept coming back to me. I wondered, *God, are You testing my faith in what I've written?* More than anything, this experience has brought me face-to-face with how difficult it is to live from a spiritual perspective while living in the material world. Even though I know how insignificant all these symptoms are to my worth, it's very difficult to live according to that knowledge. (As I write, I'm tugging on a sweater and jeans that should be much looser on me!) I wonder why these truths from my own pen (or computer keyboard) haven't sunk in deeper. How can I know this truth and still not be free?

All around me, I see both clients and loved ones tested in their self-worth too. As I try to encourage them, the words can seem so empty. How do I convince a client that she's valuable when her husband has just filed for divorce? Or when she has been betrayed by a dear friend? Or when she has just learned that her 15-year-old son is addicted to porn? What does it take to be absolutely transformed by truth, even in the face of trials?

Throughout my entire life, I've heard and believed the same panacea for what ails me spiritually: "Pray more, read your Bible more, and consider fasting." To be completely honest, when I started writing this book, I thought that's what I would suggest to you. Isn't that the formula for all spiritual growth and freedom?

The problem is that I know a lot of people who pray, read the Bible, and fast . . . and are still enslaved to masks. Jesus Himself said that when you pray, read, and fast, don't do it like the Pharisees. Although they were the most devoted to prayer, Scripture, and fasting in their culture, their spiritual disciplines did nothing to free them from their enslavement. Strangely, Jesus implied that their "solution" may have even contributed to the problem.

In my own life, I haven't found these disciplines to be entirely sufficient either. I can have my time with God and still be completely unaware of my dependence on a mask. In fact, God can even become my mask. *Hiding behind God is very different from becoming a vessel through which He shines. With one, I use God, and with the other, He uses me.*

There's no simple answer to living the truth of biblical self-esteem. It is, however, a simple problem: We're addicted to pride.

I've never experienced the full force of an addiction to shopping, eating, drinking, porn, or drugs, but I've worked with enough people who have to understand the hold it has on their lives. Almost every waking moment is spent in pursuit of the pleasure that will create euphoria; for a brief moment all the anxiety and pain will be replaced by a sense of calm and well-being.

While I don't have any of the addictions just mentioned, I do have an addiction to pride. A compliment, a success, a victory, an accomplishment—any of these can fuel me like nothing else. They fill my tank, telling me that I'm okay, that the ground I walk on is stable, and that I'm worthy of love at that moment. That "high" calls to me. How much of my life is spent in pursuit of it!

On the flip side, I fear rejection, failure, and criticism. How keenly I avoid them, as if my very survival depends upon it. If that's not an addiction, I don't know what is.

The reason no one calls pride an addiction is because it's universal. We all have it, so it can't be an illness or a sin! Sure, some mask it better than others, and it's expressed differently in various cultures. But no matter your status in life, esteemed or despised, your flesh desires pride. Adam and Eve disobeyed ultimately because they wanted to be like God.[1] Pride was the first sin of humanity and has plagued us ever since.

The addiction to pride is tricky. It comes in so many forms that we rarely recognize it for what it is: the businesswoman who ferociously climbs the career ladder; the mother whose children must appear perfect; the friend who must be needed; the wife who pouts if she isn't adored; the teacher who patronizes those who know less; the mother who can never say, "I was wrong"; the Christian who pities those who squander their lives. Pride also lives in the helpless who dream of power and status and the rejected who envy those who are loved. Pride is found not in being better than someone else but in *wanting* to be better than someone else.

PRIDEAHOLICS ANONYMOUS?

We have a slogan in my family: "All progress begins by telling the truth." It's a quote by businessman Lou Cassara that my brother came across several years ago. The concept was so helpful that it stuck, and we continue to remind each other of it through life's various challenges.

Perhaps the first step in dealing with any addiction is simply recognizing it. This sounds like a relatively simple task, but it's not. The nature of any addiction, whether it's drugs, porn, alcoholism, or you name it, is to absolutely deny that it's a problem. A 90-pound anorexic looks in the mirror and sees fat while denying food with excuses like "My stomach is just upset." The workaholic puts in 70-hour weeks only because "We have a huge case that demands a lot of time. Trust me, I don't want to work this much." The alcoholic vehemently insists, "I can stop drinking anytime I want. I'm fully in control of my desire." The same is true of pride. We'll go to any lengths to secure evidence that the "pride thing" is someone else's problem.

But we'll never conquer the mask until we admit the addiction.

"Hi, my name is Juli, and I'm a prideaholic." Pretty cheesy, right? But is there anyone in your life whom you're willing to say this to, with whom you're willing to share how desperately you seek human praise? Can you admit how jealous you are of the person who's succeeding where you've failed? Are you willing to expose how angry you become when someone doesn't give you the love or respect you feel you deserve?

Doesn't sound like such an easy step anymore. Jesus said that the road that leads to life is narrow, and very few follow it.[2] This is a narrow and treacherous road, indeed! Freedom always costs something dear; spiritual freedom is no exception.

THE ONLY TREATMENT THAT WILL WORK

The unquenchable demon of pride will keep us enslaved to our masks until the end of time. There simply is no hope, save one. There's a single answer to the problem of masks, but I guarantee you aren't going to like it. You've likely read about it in Scripture scores of times but skipped right past it because of your disdain for the word. It's more difficult to take the medicine that can free you from your mask of pride than it is for a drug addict to enter treatment. Your aversion is justified, for what God calls us to is utterly inhuman to ever desire or willfully seek.

Humility.

What Is Humility?

> *Humble 1: low or inferior in station or quality; [syn: low, lowly, modest, small] 2: marked by meekness or modesty; not arrogant or prideful; cause to be unpretentious; cause to feel shame; hurt the pride of.*
> —WORLDREFERENCE.COM, 2006

Humble and *humility* are words we regularly use in the English language. We define a *humble person* as someone who doesn't brag. A *humble background* means poverty. At least within the Christian environment, humility is an esteemed virtue that is often the result of difficult circumstances.

Because the word is commonly used, it's easy to miss the deeper spiritual concept behind what true humility is. Although I thought I understood humility, over the past several months I've begun to realize how profoundly ignorant I am of what it means to truly be humble.

Humility is *not* inferiority or self-hatred. Many people assume that a person with poor self-esteem is humble. They believe that the road to humility involves dwelling on personal inadequacies and failures. But true humility has nothing to do with feeling less valuable than anyone else. Philippians 2 highlights the fallacy of this belief. Jesus humbled Himself not because He was convinced of His inferiority but because He chose to lay aside His agenda for the will of His Father.

As we touched on much earlier in the book, inferiority and self-hatred are actually expressions of pride. Was Cain proud or humble after he presented his grain offering to the Lord? His inadequacy, jealousy, and anger were ignited by God's rejection of his offering.[3] He might have thought something like this: *Why does God reject me but bless my brother? I must not be good enough for God.* Cain's thoughts and actions were rooted in his wounded pride.

True humility frees us from the bondage of inferiority and self-loathing because it frees us from self.

Humility isn't a circumstance. Although what happens in life can humble us, circumstances by themselves don't create true humility. *Humility isn't what happens to us but what we are becoming. It isn't comprised by what surrounds us but by what emerges within us.* A poor, uneducated person can be proud, while a respected, wealthy person may be humble. Humility is an attitude of the heart, affected by circumstances but not defined by them.

My current thyroid dilemma is a circumstance that God has allowed (or maybe even brought about). The selfish part of me wants to wallow in it. "Poor me! My youth and beauty are fading before my eyes! My poor husband has to look at me every day. How can I ever write my book without energy?" On and on I can go, further into myself.

The alternative is to ask God to use this circumstance to make me humble: *Wow! I never realized how tied I am to my appearance. Lord, help me let go of my need to look beautiful and to experience the beauty of You shining through me. Give me sensitivity to others around me who feel ugly.*

Circumstances can never make me humble. They only provide the opportunity to either be immersed in self or to be emptied of self.

Humility isn't how we view ourselves; it's freedom from ourselves. Human efforts to become humble always center on changing how we think about self. We suppress thoughts of self, deny a compliment, choose to lighten up the makeup, dwell on our failures and sins, and so on. But no matter how much we change our self thoughts, we're still thinking about self. It's like that pink elephant sitting in the middle of the room. The more you tell yourself not to think about it or picture it, the more difficult it becomes to get the image out of your mind. The goal of eliminating pride in your life will simply transform it into a more acceptable form of pride. Seventeenth-century theologian William Temple said, "Humility does not mean thinking less of yourself than of other people, nor does it mean having a low opinion of your own gifts. It means freedom from thinking about yourself at all."

At the deepest levels, pride and humility are mutually exclusive. Humility is the absence of pride; pride is the absence of humility. How much of what we understand as "humility" is simply another "masquerade" of pride?

Rachel really wants to be viewed as humble. Although she lives in an upscale neighborhood, she never wears makeup, buys very modest clothing, and heads up the church's prayer chain. If you spend enough time with Rachel, you may begin to feel unspiritual in your designer jeans and Lancôme products. Her efforts to become humble have slowly become a way for her to distinguish herself from other Christian women.

Whenever we try to become humble, we'll eventually fall into the same trap as Rachel. As we quietly rejoice in our humility, our hearts secretly swell with pride.

So, How Do We Become Humble?

> *If I only had a little humility, I'd be perfect.*
> —TED TURNER

We're surrounded by things that should make us humble, yet they don't. We must sleep at least six, and preferably eight, hours every night to function. We must eat to get energy. Out of every cavity of our bodies and every pore come foul smells. Our bodies are slowly eroding to the inevitable end of death. Indeed, as the psalmist wrote, "What is man that you are mindful of him, the son of man that you care for him?"[4]

What irony! To be human means to be lowly and depraved, yet enslaved to devotion to self.

We can *never* make ourselves humble . . . "As long as we're trying to do anything, God can do nothing. It's because of our trying that we fail. We all need to come to the point where we say, 'Lord, I am unable to do anything for You, but I trust You to do everything in me.' "[5]

Perhaps the most profound truth I'm learning these days is this: Many of God's richest blessings are beyond my grasp. I can't reach them, even straining on my spiritual tippy-toes. Certainly, this is true of humility.

Not only am I addicted to pride, but I am absolutely powerless to do anything about it. I can never make myself not proud. I'm stuck inside a human spirit that detests weakness, failure, and rejection. It's sewn into the very fabric of my being.

My attempts to get rid of pride look like this: One moment, I recognize and praise God. The next moment, I congratulate myself for being such a wonderful saint! If I experience even a waking moment completely free from pride, it's only by the grace of God. The heart of the sin nature is pride, and unfortunately, I have a sin nature.

An extreme example of this is the monks who used to beat themselves with whips in order to get rid of enslavement to the flesh. Imagine whipping and cutting your body every day in order to get closer to holiness. Sounds ridiculous, doesn't it? But many of our attempts at humility are just as fruitless. *If only I read this book . . . If only I follow all of the 10 commandments . . .*

As long as I think of my faults and how unworthy I am, God will love me . . . On and on it goes; further and further we become entrenched in self.

My dear friends, we can never perform the surgery that must be done on our hearts. No amount of schooling or right-eousness can yield the fruit of humility that God so desires in His servants.

. . . but humble yourself.

This seems like a direct contradiction to the point we just discussed. How can I humble myself if I can never make myself humble?

Humility isn't something we can attain, but it is something we can both choose and seek.

When you ask the Lord to begin this work in you, you'll notice opportunities to choose humility every day. However, making the choice to humble yourself is never easy. Humility will feel painful and unnatural because it's inevitably linked with the death of a piece of yourself. When Jesus called His dis-ciples to die to self, He wasn't joking. Even in small ways, choos-ing the path of humility will be marked by feelings of dread or desperation.

Choosing the path of humility in your life today may mean not demanding your way even though it's your right to do so. It may mean being gracious to the person who cut in line or cut you off in traffic. It also means choosing to see others with the same value that you give yourself, remembering that but for the grace of God, you would be the vilest of sinners. Sometimes choosing humility is as simple and difficult as saying "I'm sorry" or refusing to become defensive in an argument.

The other day, I "fibbed" to my husband in order to avoid a conflict. It was over something very superficial, and he would likely never have discovered my indiscretion. Yet, as I spent time with the Lord that evening, I knew I had placed a wedge in my marriage and that I needed to "come clean." It took me hours of rationalizing and wrestling to muster up the courage to tell Mike the truth and confess my lie. Although it was a minor ordeal, admitting my wrong was extremely painful because it hurt my pride. I was humiliated even in the face of Mike's gracious response.

Although we can't make ourselves humble, we can desire humility and ask the Lord to cut away at our prideful hearts.

A few weeks ago, my sister Amy fell on the ice while walking her dog and shattered the bones in her left wrist. Obviously, she was in tremendous pain. Amy called 911 and was taken to the emergency room, where an orthopedic surgeon evaluated her. The doctor concluded that Amy needed immediate surgery to reconstruct her wrist with a titanium plate.

Amy knew that something was seriously wrong, but she couldn't diagnose the problem herself. She sought help from a professional. Then she had to trust the diagnosis and agree to lie unconscious on an operating table while the surgeon cut open her arm. Although she couldn't fix the problem herself, her willingness and cooperation were essential to healing.

The process of humbling ourselves is much like Amy's process of healing: *First, we must recognize we have a serious problem that's beyond our ability to fix.* Imagine how foolish it would be if Amy had tried to splint her arm and continue on with life. Or what if she had attempted to do the surgery herself using kitchen knives and dish rags? Unthinkable. But isn't this exactly what we do with our brokenness?

Second, we must seek the assistance of someone who can help. In the case of sin, there is only One who can help: the Great Physician. But calling His "number" is very difficult. Have you ever asked God to make you humble? As I'm learning to pray this prayer, I do so with great hesitation. I don't want to die to self! I don't want to let go of Juli. A sincere prayer for humility is one I know God will answer. But at what price? What will it cost me? The crossroads of Jesus' words: "For whoever wants to save his life will lose it, but whoever loses his life for me will find it."[6]

Finally, we must have faith in the Physician's goodness. What faith Amy had in a doctor she hadn't even met! She willingly accepted drugs that would make her unconscious, knowing that the doctor would cut open her arm. But what if he was inept? Or malicious? What if that doctor decided to kill or maim with his scalpel rather than heal? It's a chance Amy chose to take. The intense and constant pain and the interruption of her basic functioning made the doubt fade away.

Do I have that faith in the goodness of my Physician? Do I trust that the wounds He inflicts on me will bring about healing? Or would I rather trust in self-diagnosis and endless second opinions?

Although I can never heal myself of this pride that plagues me, my willingness is absolutely necessary. We serve a God powerful enough to rip our pride away in a split second. Yet He waits for us to ask, to seek, and to knock. And then He is caring and patient enough to prune steadily, only as much as we can handle. Slowly, He builds our faith and responds with His grace, for He knows that we are but flesh.

The Blind Will See and the Deaf Will Hear

The essence of sin is a shift from a God-centeredness to a self-centeredness. The essence of salvation is the denial of self, not an affirming of self.
—Henry Blackaby

Have you ever prayed that God would make you humble? You probably pause instinctively at the thought of doing so. Do you wonder how much of yourself He will ask for? Or what He might require that you lay down?

These are certainly questions I've asked as I count the cost of such a prayer. In my cowardly attempts to eke out a prayer for humility, I've been surprised by God's answer. *Humility comes primarily not from what God takes away from my life but from how clearly He allows me to see Him.*

God's work of revealing my brokenness isn't without purpose. Only when I've been stripped down to nothing can I see how He is everything. Likewise, when God reveals His great love and glory, my self-righteousness and entitlement disappear. *Our glory and God's glory cannot coexist in our hearts.*

There were only a few people in the Bible who came into contact with God's glory. Notice what happened in three of those accounts:

1. Moses. No other person in Scripture had more encounters with God than Moses. However, one encounter was particularly life changing. Moses asked to see the full glory of God. Because God loved Moses and was pleased with him, He said,

> You cannot see my face, for no one may see me and
> live. . . .
>   There is a place near me where you may stand on a
> rock. When my glory passes by, I will put you in a cleft in
> the rock and cover you with my hand until I have passed
> by. Then I will remove my hand and you will see my back;
> but my face must not be seen.[7]

After this encounter with the glory of God, Moses' face was so radiant that he had to wear a veil!

When God first called him to lead the Israelites out of Egypt, Moses felt inadequate. But with each encounter with God's glory, Moses became more and more confident. God's presence transformed Moses from a bumbling, doubting coward to the powerful leader who confronted Pharaoh, parted the Red Sea, and guided the Israelites through great hardship. Yet Scripture says that Moses was the most humble man "on the face of the earth."[8]

2. Isaiah. The prophet Isaiah did some pretty strange things for the Lord. He ran around naked for three years.[9] He named his children Shear-Jashub ("a remnant will return")[10] and Maher-Shalal-Hash-Baz ("quick to the plunder, swift to the spoil").[11] He was beaten and mocked while he preached without fail the absolute destruction that awaited Judah. Although some probably thought he was a crazy man, Isaiah was radically changed by an encounter he had with God:

In the year that King Uzziah died, I saw the Lord seated on a throne, high and exalted, and the train of his robe filled the temple. Above him were seraphs, each with six wings: With two wings they covered their faces, with two they covered their feet, and with two they were flying. And they were calling to one another:

"Holy, holy, holy is the LORD Almighty;
the whole earth is full of his glory."

At the sound of their voices the doorposts and thresholds shook and the temple was filled with smoke.

"Woe to me!" I cried. "I am ruined! For I am a man of unclean lips, and I live among a people of unclean lips, and my eyes have seen the King, the LORD Almighty."

Then one of the seraphs flew to me with a live coal in his hand, which he had taken with tongs from the altar. With it he touched my mouth and said, "See, this has touched your lips; your guilt is taken away and your sin atoned for."

Then I heard the voice of the Lord saying, "Whom shall I send? And who will go for us?"

And I said, "Here am I. Send me!"[12]

3. *The apostle Paul.* In chapter 2, we talked a little about Paul's transformation. He was an arrogant, self-righteous man before he met the Lord. In fact, if Paul had been around during Jesus' ministry, he probably would have been one of those Pharisees for whom the Lord had such cutting words. He may have been at Calvary mocking and jeering as Jesus hung on the cross. Instead, we find him rejoicing in a prison, chained to a wall,

probably sitting in his own filth. Great humility, yet absolutely powerful teaching.

Mary, Ezekiel, Jeremiah, and Daniel are other examples of biblical heroes who supernaturally encountered God's glory. The work the Lord set apart for each to do would have been impossible if they had trusted in the flesh. Their lives were lived contrary to all cultural expectations and pressures, yet each was able to stand in the light of knowing God.

No matter what their previous personalities or circumstances were, all were instantly and profoundly humbled by their encounters with God. It is absolutely impossible to understand God's greatness and holiness and remain proud. Andrew Murray wrote, "Humility is nothing but the disappearance of self in the vision that God is all."[13]

Jesus is the ultimate example of this. He was so filled with His Father's presence that He embodied humility. His entire purpose was to be a vessel through which God's will was done. Loving, healing, teaching, rebuking, and dying were all accomplished through the power of being filled with His Father's glory.

Also notice that true humility doesn't result in spineless groveling and kowtowing. We often think of humble people as shy and unassertive. Instead, humility means being filled with the spirit of the living God! Bold love and confident truth coexist with the meekness of knowing God's glory.

Have you ever encountered God? Do you know what it means to get even a glimpse of His holiness? When you read the Bible, pray, and fast, do you seek the face of the Savior?

Paul rejoiced at the thought of heaven because he understood that "now we see but a poor reflection as in a mirror; then we shall see face to face. Now I know in part; then I shall know fully, even as I am fully known."[14] *The transformation of seeing ourselves clearly, of having a truly accurate self-esteem, is possible only to the extent that we know and have seen God. In the quest for self-esteem, our passion must switch from the desperate search to figure ourselves out to the insatiable hunger to understand our awesome Creator in whose image we were made.*

When Losing Means Finding

He must become greater; I must become less.
—John 3:30

As a psychologist, I've often been puzzled by John the Baptist's statement regarding his role in Jesus' ministry. What does it mean for me to become less? Do people who live for God all look the same? If being holy means getting rid of self, then should holy people be like robots for God, empty shells that sing praises all day?

Instinctively, I know this can't be the case. God revels in our uniqueness. His Word is filled with godly men and women who come alive with different personalities, abilities, and characteristics. The disciples Peter and John couldn't have been more different, yet they were both consumed with Jesus.

For men or women addicted to porn, seeking a cure is frightening. It means giving up the greatest pleasure they have ever known. They often wonder who they'll be without their consuming thoughts of sexuality. The recovered addict is often amazed to find the richness of life and sexuality apart from his or her addiction. Three-dimensional love and true intimacy are so much richer than the cheap thrills that once felt so satisfying.

The same is true of pride. The self that consumes your thoughts today is a cheap imitation of the new self that the Lord longs for you to become. Have you ever met a person who is truly in love with Jesus yet lacks personality and passion? No, the opposite is always true.

Resisting our sin nature doesn't mean loss of self but the freedom of self to serve the very purpose for which it was designed. You can never fulfill the purpose of your existence until God frees you from the slavery of your pride. As you loosen your claim on life, you'll be released to be the person that God knit together in the "secret place."[15] The more of self that God prunes away, the more of the real you others can see.

Humility means losing the self that wants and demands and whines, and becoming the self that uniquely glorifies and sings and blesses.

Is It Enough?

This chapter has taken a few months to write, much longer than any other portion of this book. When I sat down to write it, I realized how ill-prepared I was to teach about humility. It's a concept I'm just beginning to get a glimpse of, much less live. At one point as I read the words of great saints like Watchman Nee and Andrew Murray, I became even more convinced that I could never write about this topic. So I put my "pen" down, prayed, and waited.

Several weeks later, I can truly say that I'm amazed. Not because I'm now humble but because God is so faithful. I can't stop crying as I see His presence and feel His hand upon me. He is so beautiful! How He answers so abundantly the pathetic prayers uttered out of a weak heart: *God, just let me see You. Let me know You deeper!*

A few weeks ago, my two-year-old son, Christian, started saying to me, "I love you so much, Mommy." I'm not sure how much he understands love; he's likely just repeating what he hears my husband and me say to him every day. Certainly his love is immature. He's self-seeking and has no concept of how to love us. Yet I treasure these sweet words in my heart. I take his toddler love and cherish it, knowing its limitations. Is this how God feels when I reach for Him? When I ask to know Him and to please Him with such imperfect prayers and such an imperfect heart?

I'm so thankful that the Lord strives with us. Like a Father, with joy, watching His child grow, He delights each time we desire to understand more of Him. At whatever level of maturity we find ourselves, He is able to use us. Still, He gently calls us to relinquish more of self every day, not simply that we may die, but that we may see Him in His glory, majesty, beauty, and the fullness of His love!

My words to you on this topic are far from perfect or even mature. But I pray that our perfect Creator will create a hunger within you to seek His presence and a humble heart. I'm striving with you, my friend, and praying that the Lord will set the captives free!

A.W. Tozer described this Father/child relationship beautifully:

How good it would be if we could learn that God is easy to live with. He remembers our frame and knows that we are dust. He may sometimes chasten us, it is true, but even this He does with a smile, the proud, tender smile of a Father who is bursting with pleasure over an imperfect but promising son who is coming every day to look more and more like the One whose child he is.

Some of us are religiously jumpy and self-conscious because we know that God sees our every thought and is acquainted with our ways. We need not be. God is the sum of all patience and the essence of kindly good will. We please Him most, not by frantically trying to make ourselves good, but by throwing ourselves into His arms with all our imperfection, and believing that He understands everything and loves us still.[16]

Surely you desire truth in the inner parts;
you teach me wisdom in the inmost place.

—PSALM 51:6

Questions for Reflection

1. What does "addiction to pride" look like in your life? What is the "fix" that you seek?

2. What do you think it means to be humble?

3. What attempts have you made at trying to be humble? What was the outcome?

4. If we can't make ourselves humble, what is our role in seeking humility?

5. What do you fear will happen if you ask God to make you humble? What keeps you from asking Him?

7

Humility Transforms Relationships

"I'm a people pleaser, and it's ruining my life." These were the first words Alissa said in counseling. She was a wife and mother in her mid-30s, owned a successful home business, and had a Palm Pilot filled with the names of friends. Yet she was lonely and angry.

As the dam of emotion broke, Alissa poured out her hurt and disappointment. Her husband was insensitive, her children were spoiled, and she felt used by almost everyone in her life. All of her friends knew that Alissa would never say no if they needed a favor. Her business was built around 24-hour customer service. Her children knew how to pull just the right strings to get what they wanted. Everyone around her seemed happy, but Alissa was exhausted and resentful of all the people "taking" from her. Yet her aversion to conflict and her need for peace kept her chained to a mask of appeasement.

Over the course of weeks, Alissa and I talked about her mask and how deeply it interfered with her relationships. At one point, I suggested that maybe others weren't taking from Alissa any more than she was taking from them. As other-centered as she appeared to be, Alissa's relationships were built around her needs for affirmation and significance. She willingly appeased her husband for the assurance of his affection. She bartered her services for the security of friendship and customers. She accommodated her children for the comfort of their approval. Her mask played a very important role in getting her needs met. So why was she unhappy?

Like Alissa, the masks we wear compromise our relationships. We keep them on because they seem to work, making life safer and more predictable. They control our deepest fears of rejection, abandonment, and chaos. Oh, how the masks promise to protect our ever-so-vulnerable self-esteem! But the security they provide comes at the great cost of demanding, lifeless, broken relationships.

As I've seen over and over again in the counseling room, significant change in relationships is difficult. No matter what we try, we just can't seem to "be" with others at a level that satisfies. We attend seminars, chasing the elusive promise of intimacy. We resolve to stop nagging, gossiping, and stuffing anger, only to fall back into the same patterns. We simply can't will ourselves to become more unselfish, more caring, and more loving.

The way we consistently act with others reveals the very depths of our hearts. Our relationships will never change until our hearts change. No self-help advice can accomplish the Holy Spirit's work. Only as humility replaces the bondage of pride and our "self-esteem pyramid" is transformed will relationships slowly and qualitatively change. This transformation must occur from the very core of our being; it's never the result of empty resolutions or willpower.

Jesus' life was the greatest example of what it looks like to live without pride and masks. His relationships weren't designed to meet His needs for worth or significance, because those needs were already met by His Father. He was free to be the hands and feet and mouth of God for others. Jesus still had friendships; He valued the companionship of Peter, James, John, Lazarus, Mary, and Martha. But He was free to love His friends without the formality of a mask or the demands of dependence.

As a woman, I can think of no sweeter fruit than God transforming my relationships. Practically my whole life is built around people: my husband, children, siblings, parents, friends, clients, and coworkers. In fact, the Bible tells me that one of my greatest purposes in life is to serve as part of the body of Christ. The painful and challenging work that God is doing within me is ultimately revealed in how I interact with others. He has purchased my freedom so that I'm able to relate with love, authenticity, and unity.

LOVE: MORE THAN A CARNATION

By this all people will know that you are my disciples,
if you have love for one another.
—JOHN 13:35, ESV

Today is February 13. You know what that means? Tomorrow is Cupid day. I remember Valentine's Eve as a young teenager. My mind was consumed with "love." If I had a boyfriend, I antici-pated the gift or words he would have for me on Valentine's Day.

Perhaps the Valentine's Day tradition I remember most from high school is the carnation sale. The week before Valentine's Day, all students were given the chance to preorder, for a dollar each, pink carnations for friends. The carnations were passed out by the cheerleaders in homeroom on Valentine's Day. What probably began as a fund-raiser turned into an obvious popular-ity contest.

I spent many February 13s of adolescence fearing that I would be one of the "rejects" who had no carnations to carry around. Would someone love me enough to pay a dollar to make my day? I could already imagine some of my fortunate friends who were "loved" so much that they would carry an armful of carnations from friends and admirers.

I wonder today how many teenagers are dreading tomorrow. Will any of them fake stomachaches to escape the proof that they are unlovable? No boyfriend or girlfriend—not even a card or carnation to express friendship. Instead of a celebration, Valentine's Day for many is only a confirmation of how utterly unloved they are.

Many of us have outgrown Valentine's Day—although it's always nice to get chocolates from our husbands! Basically, Valentine's Day is a day for elementary schools to have parties and for teenagers to celebrate puppy love and shallow friend-ships. "What do they know of love and romance?" cynical adults assert. But who are we kidding? What do we grown-ups really know about love? Isn't what we try to pass off as love as silly as the charade of conversation hearts and foil valentines?

Even as I write this, the faces of women come to mind. I think of them as one chorus imploring me to validate the logic of their "love": *Our husbands have spurned us. Our children are ungrateful. Our friends have betrayed us. So we're justified in leaving, divorcing, gossiping, hating, and taking revenge. We have fallen out of love.*

Real love isn't something we fall into and out of, because it doesn't revolve around self. Rather, it's an expression and reflection of God's incredible love for us while we were undeserving, lost, unattractive sinners! The love Jesus calls us to is so different from the nice feelings we so often assume represent love. You most likely are familiar with the biblical definition of love in 1 Corinthians 13. Here's another look at it:

> Love never gives up.
> Love cares more for others than for self.
> Love doesn't want what it doesn't have.
> Love doesn't strut,
> Doesn't have a swelled head,
> Doesn't force itself on others,
> Isn't always "me first,"
> Doesn't fly off the handle,
> Doesn't keep score of the sins of others,
> Doesn't revel when others grovel,
> Takes pleasure in the flowering of truth,
> Puts up with anything,
> Trusts God always,
> Always looks for the best,
> Never looks back,
> But keeps going to the end.[1]

Do you recognize this as love? What I learn from this passage isn't how to love but how incapable I am of love. Love as I know it is basically a reflection of myself. I love my children because they bear my image. I love my husband because he cares for me. I love my parents because of all they've given for me. I love my friends as long as they treat me well. Love as I know it is based on how other people make me feel and what they contribute to my self-esteem.

A common humanistic mantra is "You can't love others until you love yourself." I've been shocked to hear this principle repeated time and again in modern-day churches. What a distortion of truth! (Take a moment to reread the discussion in chapter 2 [pages 33–42] about what self-love really means.)

According to 1 Corinthians 13, I'll never be able to love someone else until I'm free from the love of self. *Only when I let go of my need for constant affirmation, my compulsion to be right, my awareness of how others "should" be treating me, and my demand for respect will I be able to love as Jesus loves.*

Can you imagine how different your life would be if you were capable of such love? What would it be like to walk down the street and see others through the eyes of Christ? What if Christ replaced your bitterness toward your husband, your mother, your children, or your sibling with such unconditional love?

According to the Bible, this is the hallmark of a life changed by Jesus. The greatest evidence that our lives have been transformed comes in how we love. Read what the apostle John wrote about love: "Dear friends, let us love one another, for love comes from God. Everyone who loves has been born of God and knows God."[2]

Love isn't something we try to do or endeavor to feel; it's the very presence of God shining through us, and God's presence is possible only as we let go of pride, self, and ego.

Something happened to me my senior year of high school. I stopped thinking about receiving carnations and began to consider the loneliness of others. For $10, I could buy anonymous carnations for the 10 most lonely kids in my class. I remember the secret delight I felt as I watched each of them accept a flower. Although the gesture brought momentary relief in their day, the real change was within me. Maybe I was starting to learn how to love.

GENUINENESS: THE WONDER OF NAKEDNESS

Honesty and transparency make you vulnerable.
Be honest and transparent anyway.
—MOTHER TERESA

Writing this book has turned out to be a lot more difficult than I thought it would be. Family and close friends who have looked over the manuscript have consistently had one remark: "I'm really learning about you through this book!" How could people who have lived with me for years be learning about me by what they've read in these pages?

All right. Here's one more true confession. Ever since I started writing this book, I've had a recurring nightmare about going places barely clothed. A couple of times, I dreamed that I was on a television talk show in just my bra and underwear. One time, I dreamed that I had to speak at our church on Sunday morning completely naked. To make matters worse, I had no idea what I was supposed to speak about—as if what I had to say would even matter!

As a psychologist, I'm bound to analyze my own dreams; these take little expertise to understand. Unmasking is terrifying, especially when everyone else is still clothed. Unmasking goes in tandem with humility, because what you see behind the mask is raw, unflattering humanity. However, I'm convinced of this: If the Lord is using this book in your life, it's through my genuineness, not my expertise. If you've read this far, it's because you identify with me, not because you're impressed by me. You see the hope and truth of Christ through my brokenness and sinfulness.

The power of Christ in our lives is possible only in genuineness and truth. Masks, facades, and games render us useless to His cause. Are you willing to abandon self so that the power of Christ can radiate through you?

Suppose you want to be genuine. You're checking out at the grocery store after you've just had a fight with your husband on the cell phone. The nice lady working at the cash register dutifully asks you, "How are you today?" She might as well have said, "Paper or plastic?" But remembering the need to be genuine, you rapidly explain about the argument you just had with your husband, adding, for honesty's sake, that you're PMSing. Is this genuineness? Is this what it means to live without masks?

Don't worry. Genuineness doesn't mean you have to write an exposé or tell your neighbor about your deepest, darkest secret. Being genuine means exactly that—just *being*. How you behave, what you reveal, and how vulnerable you choose to be will change based on who you're with. But all of it, whether shallow or deep, will be 100 percent authentic.

"Being" in Public—Living Truth

You probably spend a lot of time each day around people who don't really know you. You make small talk with neighbors, exchange niceties with strangers in the mall, talk about the weather with coworkers, and share the most casual of information with other moms at your child's school. These are the people who seem the most difficult to be authentic with. You don't have time for long conversations, and you're not looking for deep friendships in these situations, so what's the harm of a mask?

Even in the most casual of relationships, your mask is inconsistent with God's call on your life. God wants you to be salt in a bland world. In a group of employees or a sea of people walking down the hall, do your eyes speak of a different kind of love, healing, and forgiveness? Is your "Have a nice day" just another flat script or a heartfelt blessing?

Your life was designed to tell a story of God—a story that is hidden and disguised by the fairy tales of a mask. Although few people will ever hear your entire story, let every sentence you live be consistent with the words God is writing on your life.

Have you ever been touched by the warm eyes of a stranger or the heartfelt compassion of an acquaintance? Have you ever been drawn to the warmth or honesty of someone you hardly knew? When you refuse to participate in the masquerade, God's power can touch someone who gets even a glimpse of your story. As Peter wrote, "In your hearts set apart Christ as Lord.

Always be prepared to give an answer to everyone who asks you to give the reason for the hope that you have. But do this with gentleness and respect."[3]

Living truth also means looking past the masks of others. Do you ever care what's behind the masks of those with whom you interact casually? Are your interactions and assumptions based on superficial guideposts like appearance, job status, and facial expressions? Or do you look beyond these things, valuing each person as God's creation? Scripture reminds us that "man looks at the outward appearance, but the LORD looks at the heart."[4]

"Being" with Your Friends—Pursuing Truth

As iron sharpens iron, so one person sharpens another.
—PROVERBS 27:17, NIRV

There's a fine line between acquaintance and friendship. When does an acquaintance or coworker become your friend? It's Monday morning, and you share an elevator with a coworker. Chances are that you make small talk, asking a casual question like "How was your weekend?" You expect a true but superficial answer. "Fine." "Uneventful." "I worked in the yard." "I visited my son at college." Later in the day, you call a close friend and ask the same question, "How was your weekend?" Most likely, you're looking for a much deeper version of the truth from your friend.

Friendship means more than living and observing truth; it means *pursuing* truth. Your lives don't simply overlap and intersect. Friends are committed to, at some level, unveiling each other. But what do you pursue? Common interests? Overlapping needs? Why?

Think about two or three of your friends. When you get together with them, what do you talk about? Do you wear your mask? Do they wear theirs? Does your conversation avoid truth or encourage it?

From the world's perspective on self-esteem, our friendships are hamstrung. They can go only so deep without risking rejection. Truth is a threat to companionship and camaraderie. Many, many women come to counseling simply so they can tell and discover the truth about themselves. Even their closest friendships are marked by superficial banter and masks.

Of course, all friendships are different. Some are fun; others are serious. However, the defining characteristic of genuine friendship is truth. If your friendships lack this component, your friends are nothing more than convenient strangers. Friends gently pursue truth in each other's lives. Rather than pretend, they create environments where it's safe to be unguarded. They refuse to accept the trite "I'm doing fine" or "Same old, same old." The pursuit of truth isn't one-sided, as each friend risks being unguarded.

As God's Word has worked itself deeper and deeper into my being, I notice the difference in my friendships. For the most part, talking about Hollywood gossip or scrapbooking seems like such a waste of time. I want to connect with my friends. I want them to know me as I strive to know their hearts. Sure, there are downtimes, light conversations, and relaxing girls' nights out, but the theme of the relationships goes beyond simply sharing time and space.

"Being" with Intimates—Rejoicing in Truth

Obviously, intimate relationships are the deepest, most vulnerable relationships in our lives. You likely will have only two or three people in your lifetime who are your true intimates or soul mates.

In the worldly reality of self-esteem, unfortunately, what we often think of as "intimate" relationships are usually codependent. Two people are so intertwined with their needs for significance that each can scarcely function without the other. Like a lock and a key, their masks fit each other perfectly, feeding their needs for affirmation and self-importance.

Tina and Sharon are very close friends. Tina is a single mom barely crawling through daily life while Sharon is a mature woman whose children are grown. At the end of each day, Tina calls Sharon to voice her frustration. Sharon is the strong, calming presence that assures Tina everything will be okay. Although Sharon may not even know it, Tina's frantic phone call each night steadies her own anxiety. Through the neediness at the other end of the line, Sharon is assured that somebody needs her and she's still important.

Unfortunately, many marriages can be summed up by a similar codependency. What is intimacy beyond the deepest levels of needing someone?

Oh, the richness of intimacy that waits for us beyond the masquerade! Genuine intimates go beyond living truth and even pursuing truth in each other; they rejoice in the deepest truths.

Dana and Doug are newlyweds. They dated for more than three years and were friends long before that. At first glance, there wasn't much they didn't know about each other. So why, after six months of marriage, are they in my office arguing about toothpaste and table manners? Even on the most superficial topics, neither of them will give any ground.

Intimate relationships go beyond what friends know about each other into the realm of merging and forging together. Even good friends can accept each other's differences with little effort. At the end of the day, they go their separate ways, maintaining their independence. They don't share bank accounts, life-changing decisions, or their most vulnerable moments together. However, intimates must struggle through each conflict, annoying habit, and hurt, or they'll no longer be intimate.

Intimate relationships hold the power to satisfy us at the deepest levels of companionship. The joy of being known and accepted just as we are is unrivaled. Yet these same relationships are also the most terrifying as they represent the deepest potential for rejection and abandonment. Only when our worth is securely rooted in Christ can we risk trusting another person with oneness. Loving and connecting at this depth is too threatening when another person has the power to define our worth by his or her approval, affection, or presence.

At some point, each couple, like Dana and Doug, comes to a conclusion about their level of intimacy. Sadly, most decide that it's too threatening to be utterly unmasked by another. In fact, each will try desperately to put the mask back on when one spouse senses that the other may be too close to his or her weakness.

Once in a while, I've been in the presence of true intimates. They know each other so well that they can finish each other's sentences. In the quiet moments of life, they've shared their deepest fears, failings, and dreams. The unmasking of their souls has been met not with rejection but with love and protection. In the confines of such safety emerges the freedom to just be as they are. Intimates exchange secret glances and smiles as they rejoice in the past they share and delight in being known and loved so completely.

Freedom from the compulsive need for acceptance and affirmation from your soul mate allows you to just "be" in the presence of another who can just "be." No demands, no talking around truth, no judgment, no bitterness or keeping score. The games and masks are replaced with the joy of truly knowing and being known. Phrases like "I'm sorry" and "Please forgive me" are frequently heard as each is more invested in the relationship than in saving face.

Live the truth in public. Seek the truth with your friends. Rejoice in the truth with those few who touch your very soul. "You have made yourselves pure by obeying the truth. So you have an honest and true love for your brothers and sisters. Love each other deeply, from the heart."[5]

UNITY: DEFYING INTERPERSONAL GRAVITY

I appeal to you, brothers, in the name of our Lord Jesus
Christ, that all of you agree with one another so that
there may be no divisions among you and that you
may be perfectly united in mind and thought.
—1 CORINTHIANS 1:10

When I was in my early 20s, my dad had a heart-to-heart talk with me. "Juli," he said, "in your lifetime, there will be only a handful of people who are sincerely unified with you. Sure, you will have lots of friends, but few of them will really care. They may be nice people, but human nature is to look out for your own interests. Friends may even be jealous of your success or gloat in your failure. People you can sincerely trust are few and far between."

In the naivety of young adulthood, I was shocked by his wisdom. I thought of my good friends and wondered how they fit into this truth. I wondered about my own loyalty toward others. Was I a fickle friend too?

A primary theme in many of the Epistles is unity. Early church leaders understood the dire threat that division and competition caused to the work of Christ in believers' lives and in the church. Oh, what a heyday Satan continues to have with division among Christians! Denominations argue with one another over doctrine and tradition. Church leaders compete for money and parishioners, boasting of the newest building with the greatest amenities or the busiest social calendar. Christians regularly sue each other over worldly things. Christian friendships and churches continue to be defined by race and socioeconomic status. At the most basic level, the church has demonstrated no difference from the world, even in being unified as husbands and wives.

Jealousy, gossip, selfishness, partiality, and contention are all the natural fruits of flesh and pride. They cling to our souls like parasites. Like love and authenticity, we can't fake unity. It's a fruit that can be supernaturally evident in our hearts only as Christ frees us from the hold of pride.

Earlier in the book, we learned about the simple fact that life in masks always ends in competition. Human value is a zero-sum gain, from the world's perspective. Your value can only be determined in comparison with the value of those around you. Understanding this, it's only logical that true unity is impossible unless we're freed from the endless game of securing self-worth.

As long as establishing significance and approval is the goal, Christians will always be in competition with one another. Brother will fight brother; sister will tear down sister. Accomplishments will be measured and compared; some believers will be declared the winners, and others, the losers. Sadly, this is the state of the American church.

Think of two churches in the same small town. One is Baptist, the other Presbyterian. Both believe that Scripture is the inspired Word of God, that Jesus is the Son of God, and that salvation comes through trusting Christ. The important elements of their doctrine are identical. Although the pastors have much in common, they never speak to each other. Working on a joint community project is unheard of. They're competitors, dueling for the same souls.

Although it's more obvious when we compare churches, this same dynamic plays out in the lives of individual Christians. We bicker, backbite, gossip, and compare. We jockey for attention and hope that our gifts will be showcased. Fellow believers are more often intimidating than encouraging. It sounds like this was going on in Paul's time, based on what he wrote to the Galatian church: "But if you bite and devour one another, watch out that you are not consumed by one another."[6]

We're all at risk of forgetting who the real enemy is. Only by

*laying aside our personal agendas and rights will we stop compet-
ing and finally become useful for God's work.*

Some Christians point to 1 Corinthians 9:24 to justify their
competitive spirit: "Do you not know that in a race all the run-
ners run, but only one gets the prize? Run in such a way as to
get the prize." Doesn't this passage imply that the Christian life
is a competition to be won?

As a naturally competitive person, I used to picture myself
running a race against other Christians. In "good-natured" fellowship, perhaps we would tease each other, "Who will please
God more?" This is basically what the disciples did. More than
once in the Gospels, we find them in heated discussions about
who was winning the spiritual race.

After reading the full context of Paul's writings, we cannot
possibly think that he wanted Christians to race against one
another for a spiritual prize. Take a look at these verses:

> Rejoice with those who rejoice; mourn with those who
> mourn. Live in harmony with one another. Do not be
> proud, but be willing to associate with people of low
> position. Do not be conceited.[7]

> God has combined the members of the body and has
> given greater honor to the parts that lacked it, so that there
> should be no division in the body, but that its parts should
> have equal concern for each other. If one part suffers, every
> part suffers with it; if one part is honored, every part rejoices
> with it.[8]

> If you have any encouragement from being united with
> Christ, if any comfort from his love, if any fellowship with
> the Spirit, if any tenderness and compassion, then make my
> joy complete by being like-minded, having the same love,
> being one in spirit and purpose. Do nothing out of selfish
> ambition or vain conceit, but in humility consider others
> better than yourselves. Each of you should look not only to
> your own interests, but also to the interests of others.[9]

Competing against one another within the body of Christ is absolutely absurd. It would be like the lungs and the heart arguing about who will cross the finish line first. They'll complete the race only if they work together; they're part of the same body and the same cause! If one fails, they both lose. If one succeeds, they both celebrate.

There's only one place in Scripture where Jesus talked specifically to us as the church of the future. Here's what He prayed:

> "I pray also for those who will believe in me through their
> message, that all of them may be one, Father, just as you are
> in me and I am in you. May they also be in us so that the
> world may believe that you have sent me. I have given them
> the glory that you gave me, that they may be one as we are
> one: I in them and you in me. May they be brought to com-
> plete unity to let the world know that you sent me and have
> loved them even as you have loved me."[10]

God's desire for us is very clear. Nothing is more valuable to Him than our unity. There is to be no prejudice, favoritism, competitiveness, or dissension among believers. We're all part of *one* body, with *one* cause and *one* purpose.

Over the past few years, my husband has dabbled in marathons and triathlons. Somewhere way in the front of the race are a few superhumans running four-minute miles. But the rest of the athletes have one goal: to finish. They compete not against each other but against the course itself. In fact, throughout the race, they cheer each other on. Strangers running side by side say things like "You can do it! We're almost there!"

The race Paul ran wasn't a competitive sprint against fellow believers but an endurance race in which he needed the encouragement and help of his brothers to finish.

The Western church has little understanding of what it means to be one body, or even to be on the same team. When was the last time you wept at a fellow Christian's suffering or rejoiced in his or her triumph? Does your heart beat with or against your brothers and sisters? Are you willing to set aside your personal goals and agenda to support the work God is doing in and through them? Not just for your friends but for the unlovely and unpopular as well?

When people willingly bleed for one another, give all they have, and die for each other as the early church did, they transcend human nature. This is why the Father's work of humbling His children is so essential. Unity comes only as pride is replaced with love.

I hope and pray that the Lord is working powerfully within your heart. As His truth settles deeper and deeper within you, your life will evidence the fruits of God's love, authenticity, and unity. The change will likely be slow, maybe even imperceptible at first. But your relationships, from the most common to the most intimate, will begin to reflect the heart of our Savior.

Surely you desire truth in the inner parts;
you teach me wisdom in the inmost place.

—PSALM 51:6

Questions for Reflection

1. What impact has your mask had on your relationships?

2. In what ways does your self-love affect your ability to love other people?

3. Pick three of your relationships and describe how you could become more authentic in each of them.

4. Are there fellow Christians with whom you've felt competitive? How does your mask promote competition? What is God's desire for that relationship?

5. Why do you think unity among His children is so important to God? Why is it so difficult to achieve?

8

More Than a Job

Have you ever had a dream come true? It happened to me just this week.

As I entered young adulthood, I began to discover that God had gifted me as a communicator. Writing and speaking seemed to come naturally to me. I also started to hone in on my growing interest in Christian psychology. As I thought about what I wanted to do with my life, I considered the impact of one man in particular, Dr. James Dobson.

As a budding Christian psychologist, Dr. Dobson was a mentor from afar, communicating timeless truths with passion and wisdom. Lately, as a wife and mother, I've gained a new appreciation for the many ways that Focus on the Family ministers to and equips families. So you can imagine how I felt earlier this week when I was on Focus on the Family's daily broadcast. After decades of listening to the broadcast, it was my voice I heard on the radio. I felt as if I were in an episode of *The Twilight Zone*. I wondered, *God, how did this happen?*

As excited as I felt about being on the broadcast, the event also brought to light many of the things that the Lord is teaching me about work, ambition, and passion. In His divine plan, He has chosen to give me the desires of my heart while at the same time challenging the source of those desires. The question I keep hearing deep within my soul is this: *Juli, what do you most desire?*

Like our relationships, work is the outgrowth and reflection of the deepest longings of our hearts. As the Holy Spirit wrestles to free us from the addiction to self, our perspective and approach to work will inevitably be transformed.

Some people believe that work is a secondary issue in most women's lives, that it's really more of a man's "problem." Just look at the curse in Genesis 3:16–19. The woman's punishment revolved around relationships, while the man's curse directly related to work. But although women tend to be more relational than goal-oriented, they're still deeply affected by work.

Please understand that "work" doesn't necessarily mean a traditional nine-to-five job. Your profession may include taking care of the house, raising children, teaching a Bible study, coaching your daughter's basketball team, taking college classes, or caring for an aging parent. Every day your life is filled with some sort of work. Short of our relationships, nothing expresses and defines us more than what we do and how we do it.

I've met with countless moms who have given up their jobs in the workplace or scaled back in order to care for their children. They sometimes confess how worthless they feel without a paycheck, title, or job evaluation. I've also met with an equal number of women in the paid workforce who feel cheated out of the luxury of making Christmas cookies, volunteering at church, and attending play groups with their children. Make no mistake: Women feel incredible tension, stress, and pressure over their work. What they choose to do or not do often defines them with their friends, neighbors, family, and their church body. Their success or lack of it plays a huge role in how they feel about their self-worth and self-confidence.

"Whatever you do, work at it with all your heart, as working for the Lord, not for men."[1] This little verse, comprised of just 18 English words, contains the foundational ways in which God wants to revolutionize the way we approach every job and task. As with humility and relationships, the transformation of our approach to work goes beyond what we physically will ourselves to do. Instead, it's a renewal of our being, the very way we think about things and go about them.

There are two primary problems with all endeavors motivated by self-esteem and ego: disengagement and drivenness. They are opposite expressions of the same problem. It doesn't matter what kind of work we do; if it's rooted in the flesh, it will ultimately fall into one of these two traps.

DISENGAGEMENT: WORKING WITHOUT A HEART

Gail stomped back to her desk with an armload of papers and once again picked up the phone that had been ringing incessantly for the past five hours. "Customer relations. Can I help you?" she barked. She had become so dissatisfied with her job that she lived for five o'clock and *really* lived for the weekend when her life could once again begin.

Gail refused to think of her job as an important part of her life. It was a necessary evil that did nothing but pay the bills. Each day, she watched as the clock tediously ticked off minutes that felt like hours. When five o'clock hit, she was the first to punch out. Twenty-five minutes later, she was at home, joylessly banging pots as she made a simple supper for her husband and teenagers. Life had become drudgery.

"Whatever you do, work at it with all your heart . . ."

The essence of a disengaged approach to work is that it lacks heart. Work is viewed as something separate from who we are. Often, we take this approach when the work we're doing feels beneath us. We're embarrassed to work at the grocery store, to clean houses, or to be a stay-at-home mom who doesn't have a "job." We subconsciously reason that if we emotionally divorce ourselves from work, it won't be a reflection of who we are. It's just a "job"—something we have to do.

Another reason we detach from work is the fear of failure. We believe the lie that success and failure define personal value. So not trying becomes a safety net for defeat.

Michelle's attitude toward just about every task since adolescence could be described as halfhearted. She had perfected the art of doing just enough to get by. Even so, her natural talent, outgoing personality, and intelligence led to a modest résumé of successes. Although she enjoyed her job, she just couldn't seem to get excited about it or fully invest herself. This approach bled over into her marriage, parenting, and other relationships. Everything had become bland and passionless.

As I listened to Michelle share her frustrations of mediocrity, one phrase jumped out. Time and again Michelle said, "It's not like I really tried, but . . ." In essence, what she kept telling her-self and others was, "Don't assume that this is my best effort."

One day I asked her, "What would it mean if it *had* been your best effort?" She couldn't answer. Then I asked, "Have you ever given something your all?"

The bland expression on her face immediately melted away as she confessed that she hadn't.

As long as we hold something back, failure can be explained away by lack of effort or interest. The moment we do our work with our whole heart, we risk failing with our whole heart.

Granted, there are some jobs that are just easier to invest in. All of us have probably had jobs that we dreaded going to. Like-wise, even in the best of work circumstances, we've had those days when nothing seemed to go right and we just couldn't wait for the day to be over. However, a pattern of detachment from work indicates a wrong heart attitude.

Evidence of God's work in our lives is the supernatural abil-ity to do our work—all of our work—with passion and purpose. Work, no matter how menial or threatening, becomes no longer a reflection of our worth but a celebration of our worth and God's glory: "Don't [work only] while being watched, in order to please men, but as slaves of Christ, do God's will from your heart."[2]

DRIVENNESS: GOING FOR A DRIVE

Have you ever met a truly driven person? I meet one every day when I look in the mirror. I had ulcers (real ulcers!) as a 16-year-old worried about getting an A-minus instead of an A. I studied incessantly to make sure that my educational goals would someday become a reality. For years I had nightmares of showing up for a test unprepared. Just about everything I did I tackled with passion. Even today, I hate doing a job halfway. I don't want to attempt anything unless I'm sure I can do it right.

I used to read Colossians 3:23 with the assurance that I was one of those righteous saints who did all of my work with my whole heart. No one could ever fault me for lack of effort. What I failed to realize was that all of my passionate work, even my spiritual work, was rooted in self, not God. At the depths of my heart, it was all for the reward of praise, not for the glory of God.

My addiction to self, expressed in the quest for accomplishment, was channeled through my compulsions. To make matters even more complicated, my work was edifying and worthy of applause. I could easily justify most of it as being "for God's glory." I was applying my gifts with passion and reminded myself of verses such as "From everyone who has been given much, much will be required."³ Knowing the blessings from God on my life, I felt compelled to do great things for Him.

Throughout the past few years, I've become mindful of God working in my life in this area. This passage of Scripture hit me like a ton of bricks:

> By the grace God has given me, I laid a foundation as an
> expert builder, and someone else is building on it. But each
> one should be careful how he builds. For no one can lay any
> foundation other than the one already laid, which is Jesus
> Christ. If any man builds on this foundation using gold,

silver, costly stones, wood, hay or straw, his work will be shown for what it is, because the Day will bring it to light. It will be revealed with fire, and the fire will test the quality of each man's work. If what he has built survives, he will receive his reward.[4]

Paul was writing this to Christians. He assumed that each reader would have a trusting relationship with God, which is the foundation of all we do. However, we're building upon that foundation daily through our activity and motives. Paul tells us in Ephesians 2:10 that God saved us so that we could be His instruments, fulfilling assignments that He designed uniquely for us. Here he warns us to do that work, whatever it may be, with pure intentions.

Paul teaches us that we can be doing some very good things—evangelism, raising kids, working in the nursery, and so on—for all the wrong reasons. Likewise, we can be doing some very menial or material things—like washing dishes or selling widgets—for all the right reasons. *What we do makes very little difference compared with how we do it. God is very concerned about the motivation and purpose behind our work.*

I absolutely believe that apart from the Holy Spirit's work in our lives, it's impossible for us to do our work passionately solely for the glory of God. Again, this isn't something I can will myself to do; it must be the result of God's work, releasing the flesh so that I can truly be the Lord's vessel. However, as I mentioned before, we must invite God to do that work and pursue it with our energy and thoughts. The Lord's work of humility in our lives transfers our slavery from self to God.

As I see God doing this pruning in my life, I'm learning the importance of a few key principles as they relate to work. They are reminders that bind me to Him, prompting me to submit my motives, perspectives, and actions to Him for His glory. The slow transformation of my heart is leading to an awareness and growth in the following areas.

Finding Your Passion

People who have been freed from the tyranny of self-image are passionate. Whether they are, by personality, introverts or extraverts, they find great purpose in what they're doing.

We sometimes mistake drive for passion. Although they may appear the same on the surface, the two are actually very different. Drives invade life with inflexibility and rigidity: "My children *must* succeed academically." "I *will* become a great soloist." Passion, on the other hand, can be consuming, yet fluidly express a vision beyond self: "I'm passionate about feeding the poor." "I love helping pregnant teens." "I'm devoted to honoring God as a mom."

Our passion for work may come from two different discoveries. First is the realization of how we fit uniquely in the body of Christ. What a difference between working *with* our gifting versus working *against* it! As much as I love being a psychologist, I would be a miserable failure as a saleswoman. There's something amazing about doing what God created me to do. There are times when I teach or when I'm caring for my family that my passion is unrestrained. I love the line in *Chariots of Fire* when Eric Liddell tries to describe his passion for running: "I believe God made me for a purpose, but He also made me fast. And when I run, I feel His pleasure."[5]

Each of us has a unique passion to discover. My sister Angela loves remodeling and decorating homes. She has a knack for picking just the right paint color, furniture, and accessories. She sews curtains, refinishes furniture, and hangs wallpaper. One of her favorite things to do is to watch home-improvement shows. I love my sister, but I don't share her passion. My husband and I have lived in our home for almost four years, and we still don't have curtains. In fact, we hung up an old shower curtain in our bedroom to keep light out!

Our passions are a key component of how God has wired us and where we fit in the body of Christ. Angela has the gift of hospitality. Not only does she beautifully decorate her home, she shares it. Anytime we want, our whole family can go over to hang out or even spend the weekend. When we stay over, there are mints on our pillows, a basket of toiletries in the bathroom, and bathrobes on our beds. We wake up to the smell of a gourmet breakfast and strong coffee. When Angela stays at my house, she's lucky to get clean sheets and a bowl of cereal!

In his best-selling book *The Purpose-Driven Life*, pastor Rick Warren talks about the importance of finding our SHAPE based on spiritual gifts, heart (passion), abilities, personality, and experience.[6] When we find the sweet spot where God created us to function within His body, our work is filled with passion.

What about the person who is stuck in a job that doesn't express his or her passion? America is a unique place where we may have the opportunity to explore new job opportunities or even go back to school in midlife. Even so, most people go through their lives without ever feeling that they've found the job they were created to do. In most of the world, work is pure survival, not self-actualization.

"Whatever you do, work at it with all your heart, as working for the Lord . . ." Do you know to whom Paul wrote this verse? Slaves. Not exactly people who had the best career counseling. Paul told slaves to be passionate about their work! How is that possible?

Passion transcends finding "the perfect job" when we begin to accept that everything we do has eternal consequences. Emptying trash cans, cleaning up dog poop, changing dirty diapers, washing windows, filing papers, working for a demanding boss, answering phones—each is an opportunity to serve God with our attitude and perspective. Joyfully and diligently completing menial tasks is perhaps the greatest evidence that God's Spirit has permeated our work.

Redefining Success

If there was one message that the followers of Jesus just couldn't get, it was His redefinition of success. The prophets foretold that the Messiah would be a great King who would stop all Israel's enemies. His appearance was supposed to marshal in an unending kingdom. When Jesus' disciples followed Him, they expected greatness. They had visions of ruling with Jesus in a dynasty that would put King Solomon to shame. Yet over and over again, Jesus reframed success to them as servanthood.

Although you've probably read Jesus' teachings on servanthood before, have they transformed your thinking about work and success? If you walk into a hospital, whom do you perceive as the more successful person—the physician scrubbing for surgery or the nurse's assistant cleaning up vomit? Our natural inclination is to look at a person's level of education, salary, and position to determine importance. Jesus would answer that question based on which of them had the heart and actions of a servant. In fact, 1 Corinthians 12:22–24 teaches that the physician, as the more visible and applauded member of society, is less important than the servant who goes unnoticed and unappreciated. Does this mean that the doctor should trade in her scalpel for a mop? Probably not. Even in her role as a physician, a doctor can do the work of a servant. Her success has nothing to do with her degree, her salary, or her status but is dependent on whether she is self-serving or serves others.

Within the body of Christ, we often aspire to positions of status and respect in our work and ministries. The inherent drive for recognition and respect overrides Jesus' teaching on humility and servanthood. How difficult it is for our thinking to be genuinely transformed in this area of maturity!

A stark modern-day example of redefining success is the life of Henri Nouwen. As a young man, Nouwen was recognized as a brilliant psychologist, teacher, and writer. He quickly ascended the academic ladder, teaching at the Menninger Clinic, the University of Notre Dame, Yale, and Harvard. Then, at the height of his career, Nouwen did the unthinkable. He retired from academia to serve in a facility for the mentally handicapped.

Nouwen's drastic career change wasn't simply altruistic. As Philip Yancey wrote, "He went there not to give but to gain, not

out of excess but out of need. He went in order to survive."[7]
Read Nouwen's own words regarding his decision:

> I might once have held the illusion that one day the many
> bosses would be gone and I could finally be the boss of
> myself. But this is the way of the world in which power is
> the main concern. . . . Spiritual fatherhood has nothing to do
> with power or control. It is a fatherhood of compassion. . . .
> Can I give without wanting anything in return, love without
> putting any conditions on my love? Considering my immense
> need for human recognition and affection, I realize that it
> will be a lifelong struggle. But I am also convinced that each
> time I step over this need and act free of my concern for
> return, I can trust that my life can truly bear the fruits of
> God's spirit.[8]

How clearly the definition of success was turned on its ear
for Henri Nouwen!

Releasing the Spoils of War
John Wesley said,

> I do not see how it is possible, in the nature of things, for
> any revival of religion to continue long. For religion must
> necessarily produce both industry and frugality, and these
> cannot but produce riches. But as riches increase, so will
> pride, anger, and love of the world in all its branches. . . . Is
> there no way to prevent this—this continual decay of pure
> religion?[9]

This quote sums up an undeniable problem of humility. As our work is rooted in and devoted to God, we'll often experience material success. Those triumphs and the rewards they'll likely bring can lure us back into the flesh.

Our culture is filled with churches and universities founded on humbly fulfilling God's calling. As these ministries were blessed by God, they grew. But as they prospered, many of them abandoned the godly dependence that made them great. America itself is a prime example of this.

So, in our lives and our work, how do we avoid this trap? If God blesses our work, our families, and our ministries, how do we stay humbly connected to the Shepherd? How do we avoid the trap of taking the glory away from the only One who deserves it?

Second Samuel 8 tells the story of King David's amazing military success and attributes his success to God: "The LORD gave David victory wherever he went."[10] The story also reveals a key to David's humility, in spite of his outrageous victories. He immediately dedicated all the gold, silver, and bronze to the Lord. He refused to accept for himself the most precious spoils of war.

Although terms like "the spoils of war" seem pretty far from our reality, don't miss the principle. Just about every day, we receive rewards for what we do. It may be a paycheck, a compliment, a testimony of a life that we touched, or even a child that happened to behave that day. When our work is ego-driven, we automatically claim the loot we "earned." We roll around in the praise and congratulate ourselves on the success.

When our work is God-inspired, we waive the right to our

treasures. *Even though the paycheck goes into our bank account and the praise encourages our spirit, we release our claim on them.* Tithing is certainly a practical way of doing this, but what David did went far beyond tithing. He acknowledged by his actions that the victory was God's; he was just an instrument.

One day, my work is dedicated to God; the next day, it's all about me. It's a constant struggle. For me to remain an instrument in God's hand, I must find a way to daily release the spoils of war, or they're sure to capture my wandering heart.

Honoring the Sabbath

"Remember the Sabbath day by keeping it holy."[11] Of all the Ten Commandments, this is the one I least understand. Are we as Christians supposed to keep this commandment? If so, how? If not, why is this commandment different from the other nine? For many years, I didn't even know that the Sabbath was actually Saturday. I always assumed it was Sunday, since that's the day Christians set aside as "different."

Throughout my Christian life, I've been in churches that teach very different views of the Sabbath (or Sunday) and what it means to keep it holy. The debate isn't a new one. In fact, it was one of the topics Jesus and the Pharisees argued about. Jesus said, "The Sabbath was made for man, not man for the Sabbath."[12]

I've settled on the fact that how I honor the Sabbath is a matter of conscience, but honoring it is a matter of obedience. Whether I set aside Saturday or Sunday, taking a weekly break from work is both God's gift to me and my gift to Him. It's a critical discipline in keeping a God-focused perspective on my work.

The first time I really took seriously the idea of Sabbath rest was in college. I've already told you how driven I was about grades. One semester, God's Spirit began to convict me about studying on Sundays. This particular semester, I was taking 16 credit hours and playing on the varsity tennis team. Between classes, 3 hours of tennis practice a day, and traveling for matches on the weekends, I needed every spare moment of studying I could get. How could I give up Sundays? "Trust Me" was the Lord's answer.

In faith, I made the commitment not to do any schoolwork on Sundays. No papers, no studying for tests, no reading for classes. While many of my classmates crammed for Monday exams, I worshiped, took walks, napped, and spent time with friends. To my amazement, that was the first semester I earned straight A's! Although I did my part working hard the other six days, I believe those grades were largely due to God's honoring my faithfulness to Him.

Through regularly resting from our work, we acknowledge our limitations. It's a constant reminder that we're far more dependent on God than we know. It's a tithe of our time, placing faith in the fact that all blessings come ultimately from God's hand, not from our striving. Because of His faithfulness, the world keeps on turning when we stop working. He gives to His beloved even in their sleep.

Following the Voice of the Shepherd

Before even making it to the couch in my office, Melissa blurted out, "God told me to quit my job tomorrow." She was a school-teacher, and it was February.

"Okay, tell me about it," I said, trying to figure out how to respond.

Melissa explained that she had been watching television the night before, when a thought popped into her head. She was convinced that the thought was God's voice telling her to find a new profession.

"Is there any moral or ethical reason why you should quit?" I asked.

"No," Melissa replied.

"Do you have a contract with the school?"

"Yes. It ends in June."

"Do you have a plan for a different job?" I probed.

"No, I just know that I'm supposed to quit now—not wait until June. I'm sure God will tell me the rest later."

Interchanges like this one make me very leery of saying, "Follow God's voice." Throughout my years as a counselor, I've had people claim that God told them to get a divorce, have an affair, give money to a political candidate, and even paint their house a different color. How can I argue with that? Who am I to say whom God is speaking to or what He's saying?

So before we get into this, let me make one thing very clear: God never contradicts Himself. The primary way God speaks to us is through the Bible. He will never place on our hearts an instruction that contradicts the truth in His revealed Word. We have to be very careful not to assign God's name to our feelings, attitudes, and beliefs. Having clarified that, remember that we serve a living God who is active in our hearts. As His Spirit replaces the ego that drives us, His leading in our work becomes essential.

Henry Blackaby's timeless study *Experiencing God* applies this principle to our lives. He challenges Christians to reorient our passion and energy around what *God* is doing rather than asking God's blessing on what *we* want to do:

> We do not sit down and dream what we want to do for God
> and then call God in to help us accomplish it. The pattern
> in Scripture is that we submit ourselves to God and we wait
> until God shows us what he is about to do or we watch to
> see what God is doing around us and join Him.[13]

Although God may be working within us, His work does *not* revolve around us. Our job is to direct our work around what God is doing, not to demand that He conform His work around what *we* are doing. This is a critical shift in thinking that must change as we get away from the bondage of self.

God communicates His will to His children, and He wants us to join Him in His work. The quintessential question becomes, "How do we find God and hear His voice?"

Jesus said to His disciples:

> "He calls his own sheep by name and leads them out. When
> he has brought out all his own, he goes on ahead of them,
> and his sheep follow him because they know his voice. But
> they will never follow a stranger. . . .
>
> "I am the good shepherd; I know my sheep and my
> sheep know me. . . .
>
> "My sheep listen to my voice; I know them, and they
> follow me."[14]

The only way to recognize the Shepherd's voice is to have an intimate relationship with Him. The other day, I was in the grocery store, lost in the world of reading labels and comparing prices on canned soup. Even though the store was filled with noises and voices, I distinctively heard the faint voice of my husband in the distance. His voice is seared into my consciousness. I hear it every day in conversations, whispers, and playful banter. He is my intimate. I can pick out his voice among thousands of others.

The same is true of the voice of God. The more intimate we are with Him and the more often we talk and listen to Him, the more readily we'll distinguish His call amid the cacophony of voices. Jesus, as always, is our example. He deliberately, regularly sought time alone with His Father. When times of temptation and decision faced Him, He could immediately discern His Father's voice from other voices, even friendly ones.

Think of the story of Jesus and Peter. Jesus was explaining to His disciples what was going to happen to Him in the near future. His good friend Peter tried to comfort Jesus by saying, "Never, Lord! This shall never happen to you!"

Jesus might have responded to His friend, "Thanks for the encouragement, Peter. I hope it doesn't happen too." Instead, He turned to Peter and said, "Get behind me, Satan! You are a stumbling block to me; you don't have in mind the things of God, but the things of men."[15]

There are so many voices, even good voices, that easily drown out the call of our Shepherd. *The voices of "Satan" may even be from our closest friends or family members who genuinely* have our best interests at heart. Only with attentive ears toward the Shepherd can we discern the things of God from the things of people.

"Lord, what would You have me do? I am Yours."

The day my Focus on the Family broadcast aired, a dear friend sent me an encouraging e-mail. She wrote, "Keep pressing on toward your dream and bless all of us in so doing." Her words struck a chord deep within me. What was my dream? What was I pursuing?

As God is removing my masks and shining His light on my pride, I realize how my old dreams need to die. As He called Abraham to put his promised son on the altar, so must I let go of the visions and dreams that have been the source of my drive. There's only one dream to which God is calling me: being His servant today. I don't know what His call on my life will look like tomorrow or the next day. All I know as a sheep is that the only passion for me is listening to the voice of my Shepherd. If I wander into other pastures, even ones that look fruitful, I wander at my own peril.

I ask you, my friend, what voices within and around you do you follow in your endeavors? Are you free to pursue the passion of godliness, doing your work heartily as for the Lord and not for people?

Surely you desire truth in the inner parts;
you teach me wisdom in the inmost place.

—PSALM 51:6

Questions for Reflection

1. How are drivenness and disengagement different extremes of the same problem? Which one do you tend to struggle with?

2. How would you approach work differently if you were free from your masks?

3. To what degree does your work reflect your passion? What is the difference between passion and drive?

4. How do you think Jesus would define *success* in your job? How is that definition different from how you view success?

5. How would honoring the Sabbath affect your approach to work?

6. What does it mean to listen to the voice of the Shepherd? How can you tune your heart to listen to Him and recognize His voice?

9

This Is My Story . . . This Is My Song

Recently, I was at a social gathering and sat beside someone I knew only casually. We played on the same summer tennis team and said "Hi" whenever we saw each other, but we had never really talked. As soon as I sat down, I said, "Tell me about yourself."

So much for icebreakers—I think I caught her off guard. She fumbled around a little bit and then asked, "What do you want to know?"

I replied, "I'd like to know your story."

Everyone's life tells a unique story. Even the simplest, most boring life has within it a profound tale. The moment we begin talking to people, we start hearing their stories and telling them ours. We may discuss the peripheral details, such as where we live, whether we're married, and what baseball teams we cheer for. Only rarely do we volunteer the true narrative of our lives.

The masquerade is all about protecting our story—telling fiction rather than truth. We alter the facts, leaving out unflattering details and embellishing our own importance in the story line. Over time, we convince ourselves of the fiction we tell and retell until the mask feels more genuine than the truth.

Every day, you tell your story to strangers, coworkers, neighbors, children, friends, and your spouse if you're married. What story do you tell? Is it a comedy? A romance? A tragedy? Who are the heroes and villains? Most important, is your story the fiction of a mask or the truth of brokenness and dependence on Christ?

THE KING OF FICTION

Satan himself masquerades as an angel of light.
—2 CORINTHIANS 11:14

The Bible refers to Satan as the "father of lies."[1] As much as the Lord delights in truth, Satan delights in fiction. Don't get me wrong; I love a great novel as much as anyone. Some of the most powerful books I've read have been fiction. In fact, Jesus told fictional stories, such as the prodigal son, to teach timeless truths. However, He never *confused* the truth with fiction.

Satan, on the other hand, craftily weaves together truth and lies. As he works in your life, he doesn't tempt you to completely fabricate the details of your narrative. Instead, he entices you to alter your story line ever so slightly from the truth that would bring God glory.

Luke chronicles the events of a couple who gave in to the temptation of wearing a mask. The early church was so on fire for God that the members shared all of their resources with one another. A husband and wife, Ananias and Sapphira, decided to sell a piece of their property and donate the proceeds to the church. What began as a generous gesture was soon twisted into fatal fiction. The couple claimed that they sold the land for a smaller amount than they actually received. They weren't obligated to give any of the money to the church, but they lied about the amount of their donation to appear more spiritual than they really were. Here's what happened next:

> Then Peter said, "Ananias, how is it that Satan has so filled
> your heart that you have lied to the Holy Spirit and have kept
> for yourself some of the money you received for the land?
> Didn't it belong to you before it was sold? And after it was
> sold, wasn't the money at your disposal? What made you think
> of doing such a thing? You have not lied to men but to God."
> When Ananias heard this, he fell down and died.[2]

There is no halfway. When we claim to be Christians and call Jesus "Lord," everything we have belongs to Him. We either live for ourselves or identify with Christ. *Satan will do everything within his power to twist together truth with fiction and pride with righteousness as we sing our life song. We must never believe the lie that we can pursue both self and God.*

ALL I HAVE TO OFFER

I vividly remember seeing Mel Gibson's *The Passion of the Christ.* As I watched the compelling rendition of what Jesus did for me on the cross, the only thought that went through my mind over and over again was, *Lord, nothing I could give You would ever be too much.*

The greatest thing I can give Jesus is my story. Luke records the story of Jesus healing a man of many demons. The man was so grateful that he begged to follow Jesus as His disciple. "But Jesus sent him away, saying, 'Return home and tell how much God has done for you.' So the man went away and told all over town how much Jesus had done for him."[3]

For many of us, following the Lord means returning home to tell others of the great things God has done for us. To be the Lord's disciples, we must be willing to let go of our most precious possessions—our stories—the past, the present, and the future. Will we tell the real story or will we cling to a whitewashed version that makes us look okay but dilutes the significance of Christ's work in our lives?

Jesus, Be the Keeper of My Past

When I look at the stories of people in the Bible, they aren't exactly flattering. Sure, a few heroes emerge, but even their faults are exposed. Take David, for example. God repeatedly referred to him as His faithful servant and the apple of His eye. But how would David feel to know that billions of people throughout history have read about his most intimate sins?

Christians and Jews for all time remember David not only as a great king and musician but also as an adulterer and murderer.

Often, our reluctance to abandon the masquerade is based on our unwillingness to surrender the past to God. Your history may contain tragic scenes like sexual abuse, divorced parents, promiscuity, abortion, rejection, and failure. Isn't it wise just to leave all that behind? Paul himself spoke of "forgetting what is behind and straining toward what is ahead."[4]

It's certainly counterproductive to live in the past or to characterize ourselves by what happened yesterday. The transforming work of God in our lives makes us new creatures. Indeed, the old things in our lives have passed away, and "all things have become new."[5] So why are David's sins chronicled for all of humanity to study? Why must we know about the ugly things that people do or that happen to them—Sarah's manipulation, Rahab's prostitution, Tamar's rape, and Peter's denial?

When we truly surrender our self-esteem to God, we give Him the fullness of our stories to use as He wills. Our past no longer defines us; instead, it tells the great story of God's grace and mercy as He has redefined us.

Imagine if Corrie ten Boom had decided that it would be too traumatic to retell the story of her terror and loss during the Holocaust. We can only imagine how many people wouldn't know God today if she had refused to tell her story. When your story belongs to God, you trust Him with your past, not simply to heal from it and bury it, but to tell of it when He calls you to. Every difficult and painful event in your life can be used to glorify God and tell others of His great love.

Have you given God free rein to use the story of your past? Like the woman at the well and the man possessed by demons, are you humble enough to proclaim what God has set you free from?

Jesus, Be the Author of Today

Many Christians have no problem telling the world about the sin God saved them out of. They tell gut-wrenching stories of drugs, addiction, and sex from their pasts, but far more terrifying would be sharing the truth about who they are today.

It's acceptable within the Christian subculture to have a sordid past. Jesus has brought all kinds of sinners to the well of living water. However, once you've taken a sip, sin and depravity are no longer tolerated.

We doggedly cling to the lie that God's children are totally released from sin, confusion, and doubt. Why do we believe this when Scripture tells us over and over again that we'll struggle with temptation and fleshly desires as long as we have breath?

Joe and Deanna had been on a very rough ride throughout their 20 years of marriage. In fact, they separated twice and seriously contemplated divorce within the first decade of their lives together. But through prayer and hard work, they learned to love each other and resolve their most significant conflicts. About five years ago, they were asked to head up the marriage-mentoring program at their church. Eager to share what they had learned, they enthusiastically agreed.

But unresolved conflicts over credit-card bills and problems in the bedroom resurfaced, and now Joe and Deanna are barely on speaking terms. In public, they smile and even hold hands. None of the young couples they meet with would ever guess the inward rage they feel toward each other. How could they ever admit to their struggles when so many people look up to them? They're stuck in a plastic fairy tale.

Although leadership and mentoring are important, we have to be careful about assuming that any believer is beyond struggle or temptation. The greatest leaders, like Paul, are those who are constantly accountable and honest about their weaknesses. This is why Jesus taught,

> "You are not to be called 'Rabbi,' for you have only one Master and you are all brothers. And do not call anyone on earth 'father,' for you have one Father, and he is in heaven. Nor are you to be called 'teacher,' for you have one Teacher, the Christ. The greatest among you will be your servant."[6]

We give Satan the victory when we don't tell ourselves and others the truth about who we are today. We look around the church and assume that other Christians don't have doubts, don't gossip, and aren't battling addictions. So we pretend to be strong and victorious.

The church fails to reach a broken world because we refuse to admit our own frailty. *Releasing your story to God means surrendering the truth about today—how you struggle, what you fear, and the thoughts you battle. Remember, only through your weakness can the true story of God's glorious power be told.*

What a compelling example Joe and Deanna would be for young couples if they modeled their vulnerability and dependence on God! Although it wouldn't be appropriate to share all the nitty-gritty details of their conflict, they would have a far more powerful impact on young couples if they would model what it is to be an older couple in the thick of seeking God through disappointment. The world (and the church) is full of people who pretend to have it all together. Where are the models of those who cling to God in the midst of their fallenness?

Today is the most difficult day to be genuine, because it's the present. Yet today, in this moment, is the only time in which you can truly be authentic. Yesterday is history, and tomorrow is just a thought. Is Jesus the Author of your life today?

Jesus, Be the Composer of My Future

How would you live if you knew you would die tomorrow? Most likely, today would be the most authentic and genuine day of your life. You would openly grieve your regrets and extravagantly express your feelings toward others. It would be a day of canceling debts, confessing grudges, and celebrating love. You wouldn't talk about the weather or your grocery list; your words would be carefully chosen to most accurately reflect the depth of your heart. So what's holding you back from living like that today?

Tomorrow.

Expressing the nakedness of your heart today means that you could never again hide in the same way. You could no longer withhold your vulnerable feelings or control how others perceive you. Your true self would be exposed for anyone to exploit.

The story of your future is much safer and more predictable behind your mask. By projecting a friendly image, you can be sure to have friends tomorrow. By reminding others of your credentials, you can cling to the security of your success story. By portraying the victim, you can rally the troops around you. By playing the rescuer, you can script a part of importance in the screenplay of your life.

What if you truly signed over the copyrights of your future to God? Imagine if you absolutely depended on Him for tomorrow, abandoning your claim to what you desire? How would your story change?

With all its books of history, law, poetry, proverbs, songs, prophecy, and encouragement, the Bible has one main theme: to tell a story. God's Word is filled with biographies. From Adam and Eve to the apostles, we see thousands of stories unfold in the pages of Scripture. Just think of them: Samson, Job, Uzziah, Jeremiah, Noah, Herod, King Saul, Esther, Hosea. We don't even know the names of many of the characters. Thousands of years after they lived, their names are barely important. Each life is unique and essential not because of who the person was but because of the part he or she played in telling the only story that matters—the story of God. In fact, the Bible is composed of nothing more than thousands of stories, all reflecting the overarching story line of God's relationship with humanity.

The masquerade is the ultimate form of idolatry. Worshiping masks to establish safety and importance in this earthly realm robs God of what He created us for: to tell the story of His glory.

The most profound sacrifice you have to give God is total access to your story. Every time you choose to put on a mask, you compromise your offering. The love of Jesus has freed you from the game of the masquerade to make you His. He has purchased your story. The highest level of abandonment is releasing the rights to create, interpret, and plan your story.

And so, my friend, you face the same choice I do: As you prepare for today, will you put on your mask and play the games of this world, or will you embrace with humility the story of our Creator and Lord?

As you search for value, significance, meaning, and love throughout your life, you need look no further than the story of a Savior who knows each of your thoughts, numbers the hairs on your head, and designed you uniquely to love and glorify Him. This is your story . . . this is your song. Tell it over and over again. Sing it to your children, to your friends, to the lost and lonely whom God brings across your path. This is life beyond the masquerade!

In a loud voice they sang:
"Worthy is the Lamb, who was slain, to receive power
and wealth and wisdom and strength and honor and
glory and praise!" Then I heard every creature in
heaven and on earth and under the earth and on the sea,
and all that is in them, singing: "To him who sits on
the throne and to the Lamb be praise and honor and
glory and power, for ever and ever!"

—REVELATION 5:12–13

Questions for Reflection

1. How does your mask protect your story (and your reputation)?

2. Why is your story the greatest gift you have to give the Lord?

3. How are masks the ultimate form of idolatry?

4. What is the most difficult for you to do: let Jesus be the Keeper of your past, the Author of your today, or the Composer of your future? Why?

Notes

Introduction

1. John 15:2.

Chapter 1

1. *The Phantom of the Opera,* produced by Andrew Lloyd Webber, lyrics by Charles Hart, music by Andrew Lloyd Webber. Based on the 1909 novel by Gaston Leroux. Opened on Broadway January 26, 1988.
2. *The Breakfast Club,* directed by John Hughes, Universal Pictures, 1985.
3. Matthew 7:26–27.
4. Matthew 19:21.
5. Matthew 9:12–13.
6. Hebrews 4:13, 15–16.
7. John 15:18–20.
8. Galatians 1:10, HCSB.
9. John 13:34–35.
10. 1 Corinthians 9:24.
11. Isaiah 64:6.

Chapter 2

1. *The Matrix,* directed by Andy Wachowski and Larry Wachowski, Warner Brothers Pictures, 1999.
2. C. S. Lewis, *The Screwtape Letters* (Grand Rapids: Revell, 1979).

3. Ephesians 6:12.
4. 1 Peter 5:8.
5. John 8:44, HCSB.
6. Psalm 51:17.
7. Mark 12:31.
8. 2 Timothy 3:2–5.
9. Philippians 2:4, 20–21.
10. John 14:6.
11. 1 John 2:15–17.
12. Acts 9:4.
13. Philippians 3:4–9, NKJV.
14. Hebrews 11:6.

Chapter 3

1. Jeremiah 17:9.
2. 1 John 4:10.
3. Ephesians 3:17–19.
4. Psalm 118:29.
5. Jay Leno, "Oprah's Cut with Jay Leno," interview by Oprah Winfrey, *O Magazine,* February 2003, http://www.oprah.com/omagazine/200302/omag_200302_ocut.jhtml.
6. James 1:8.
7. Hosea 12:11.
8. Matthew 25:30.
9. Romans 3:12.
10. Lamentations 4:2.
11. Alexandre Dumas père, *The Man in the Iron Mask* (New York: Tor Books, 1998).

12. 1 John 3:10.
13. Matthew 5:13.
14. Henri J. M. Nouwen, *The Return of the Prodigal Son* (New York: Doubleday, 1992), 40.

Chapter 4

1. Thomas Merton, *Essential Writings* (Maryknoll, NY: Orbis Books, 2000), 55–56.
2. *Harvard Review of Psychiatry*, cited in Harvard Medical School, "Dropping Out of Psychotherapy," *Harvard Medical School Family Health Guide*, October 2005 update, http://www.health.harvard.edu/fhg/updates/update1005d.shtml.
3. Matthew 23:27–28.
4. Henri J. M. Nouwen, *The Return of the Prodigal Son* (New York: Doubleday, 1992), 20–21.
5. Ecclesiastes 9:2.
6. Romans 6:16, 18.
7. 1 Corinthians 12:26–27.
8. 1 Corinthians 4:7.
9. Nouwen, *Return of the Prodigal Son*, 43.
10. 1 Corinthians 12:7.
11. 2 Corinthians 12:9.
12. 1 Corinthians 1:27–28.
13. Romans 5:8.
14. Dr. Larry Crabb, "What Do You Desire More Than God?" (sermon, Fellowship Bible Chapel, Chagrin Falls, OH, September 5, 2005).

Chapter 5

1. Charles J. Sykes, *Dumbing Down Our Kids: Why American Children Feel Good About Themselves but Can't Read, Write, or Add* (New York: St. Martin's Press, 1995), cited in Frank Stephenson, "For the Love of 'Me,'" *Research in Review* (Summer 2004): 24, http://www.rinr.fsu.edu/summer2004/summer2004.pdf.
2. Watchman Nee, *Secrets to Spiritual Power* (New Kensington, PA: Whitaker House, 1998), 32.
3. Henry T. Blackaby and Claude V. King, *Experiencing God Workbook* (Nashville: Lifeway Press, 1990), 18.
4. Philippians 4:13.
5. Romans 8:28.
6. 1 John 5:15.
7. Romans 8:37.
8. Genesis 21:22, HCSB.
9. Mark 8:34.
10. 1 Samuel 10:21–22.
11. 1 Samuel 13–14.
12. 1 Samuel 13:13–14.
13. Matthew 19:21.
14. Mathew 19:24.
15. Watchman Nee, *Secrets to Spiritual Power*, 27, 30.

Chapter 6

1. Genesis 3:1–6.
2. Matthew 7:14.
3. Genesis 4:4–8.

4. Psalm 8:4.

5. Watchman Nee, *Secrets to Spiritual Power* (New Kensington, PA: Whitaker House, 1998), 25.

6. Matthew 16:25.

7. Exodus 33:20–23.

8. Numbers 12:3.

9. Isaiah 20:3.

10. Isaiah 7:3.

11. Isaiah 8:3.

12. Isaiah 6:1–8.

13. Andrew Murray, *Humility: The Journey Toward Holiness* (Minneapolis: Bethany House, 2001), 63.

14. 1 Corinthians 13:12.

15. Psalm 139:13–15.

16. A. W. Tozer, *The Root of the Righteous* (Camp Hill, PA: Christian Publications, 1955).

Chapter 7

1. 1 Corinthians 13:4–7, MSG.

2. 1 John 4:7.

3. 1 Peter 3:15.

4. 1 Samuel 16:7.

5. 1 Peter 1:22, NIrV.

6. Galatians 5:15, ESV.

7. Romans 12:15–16.

8. 1 Corinthians 12:24–26.

9. Philippians 2:1–4.

10. John 17:20–23.

Chapter 8

1. Colossians 3:23.
2. Ephesians 6:6, HCSB.
3. Luke 12:48, NASB.
4. 1 Corinthians 3:10–14.
5. *Chariots of Fire,* directed by Hugh Hudson, Warner Brothers Pictures, 1981.
6. Rick Warren, *The Purpose-Driven Life: What on Earth Am I Here For?* (Grand Rapids: Zondervan, 2002).
7. Philip Yancey, *Soul Survivor: How Thirteen Unlikely Mentors Helped My Faith Survive the Church* (New York: Doubleday, 2001), 296.
8. Henri Nouwen, *Return of the Prodigal Son* (New York: Doubleday, 1992), 127–28.
9. John Wesley, dated 1786, quoted at http://www.world ofquotes.com.
10. 2 Samuel 8:14.
11. Exodus 20:8.
12. Mark 2:27.
13. Henry T. Blackaby and Claude V. King, *Experiencing God: How to Live the Full Adventure of Knowing and Doing the Will of God* (Nashville: Broadman and Holman, 1998), 28.
14. John 10:3–5, 14, 27.
15. Matthew 16:23.

Chapter 9

1. John 8:44.
2. Acts 5:3–5.